Canva User Guide For Beginners

Design Stunning Graphics for Social Media, Business, and More

Clara Caden

Disclaimer

This book is intended for educational purposes and practical guidance only. While every effort has been made to present accurate, current, and easy-to-follow instructions, please note that software tools like Canva evolve quickly. Features, menus, tool names, pricing, and licensing terms may change after publication. Always check Canva's official documentation and on-screen prompts for the most up-to-date information before making important decisions. The author and publisher are not responsible for any loss, damage, or claims arising from the use of this book's content.

Stock images, fonts, music, videos, and graphic elements each have their own licenses. Examples used in this book are for demonstration purposes only. Before you sell, distribute, or publicly use a design, ensure that every asset in the design is appropriately licensed for its intended use. Canva's licensing terms and third-party licenses should be reviewed and followed. Printed colors and screen displays may not match perfectly due to differences in paper, printer calibration, and export settings. Always perform a small test print or proof to confirm results before finalizing a project.

When creating designs, be mindful of personal data, intellectual property, and applicable copyright laws. Brand names, logos, and trademarks used in designs belong to their respective owners. No endorsement or affiliation with any third-party brands is implied by the use of their logos or trademarks in any design.

Accessibility guidance provided in this book is intended to assist with general design principles but does not replace a formal accessibility audit. If your project requires compliance with specific standards (such as WCAG), engage a qualified professional to review your work. The author and publisher provide this book "as is," without warranties of any kind, express or implied.

Table of Contents

Chapter 1: Introduction

Canva changed how people think about design. Before it, professional tools like Photoshop or Illustrator demanded skill, time, and often expensive licenses. Canva broke that barrier. It gave non-designers a way to create polished graphics without the steep learning curve. But here's the catch—most users only explore the surface. They drag, drop, and download, unaware that Canva's deeper layers can transform how they think about visual communication. This guide exists to close that gap. It's not about making prettier posts; it's about understanding design as a language—and using Canva fluently.

What Canva Is and Why It Matters

Canva sits in a unique spot between design software and productivity tools. It doesn't compete head-to-head with programs like Photoshop or Illustrator, which focus on precision and complex editing. Instead, Canva centers on accessibility. It's built for quick iteration, collaborative work, and visual storytelling across formats—social media graphics, presentations, reports, invitations, and even videos.

While Photoshop users adjust layers and masks, Canva users drag and align. The difference isn't about quality but intent. Canva works when speed and clarity matter more than advanced manipulation. A marketing associate can create branded slides in minutes. A teacher can design classroom materials that look professionally made. Small business owners rely on it for flyers, menus, and online ads. Even corporate teams use Canva to maintain visual consistency across departments.

What sets Canva apart isn't just ease—it's adaptability. Its growing template library reflects how people communicate today: visually, fast, and across multiple platforms. Canva also evolves with trends, integrating tools for video, animation, and AI-driven design suggestions. It stays relevant because it bridges creativity and practicality. It doesn't ask users to be artists. It helps them think visually, which is what modern communication requires.

How This Guide Will Help

This guide teaches more than how to use Canva—it builds design sense. Each chapter moves beyond "click this button" instructions to unpack why those actions matter. Understanding spacing, hierarchy, and contrast helps anyone create designs that communicate clearly. The goal isn't to memorize features but to think like a designer using Canva as the medium.

The chapters progress deliberately. The first section introduces the core tools: workspace layout, templates, and customization options. The next dives into design principles—color, typography, and alignment—and how they apply inside Canva. Later chapters explore practical projects, from brand kits to presentations, to show how small choices affect results. Readers finish with confidence not just in using Canva, but in designing with intention.

This isn't a guide for mastering every feature or integration. It doesn't cover advanced workflows, API connections, or automation tools. Instead, it focuses on what most creators need daily: how to translate ideas into visuals that work. Each concept builds toward practical understanding, not software mastery.

The bigger idea is simple: design isn't mysterious. It's built on structure, rhythm, and logic—patterns that anyone can recognize and apply. Canva just happens to make those patterns visible. With the right mindset, it stops being a "template app" and becomes a creative workspace where clear thinking meets clean design.

Chapter 2: Getting Started with Canva

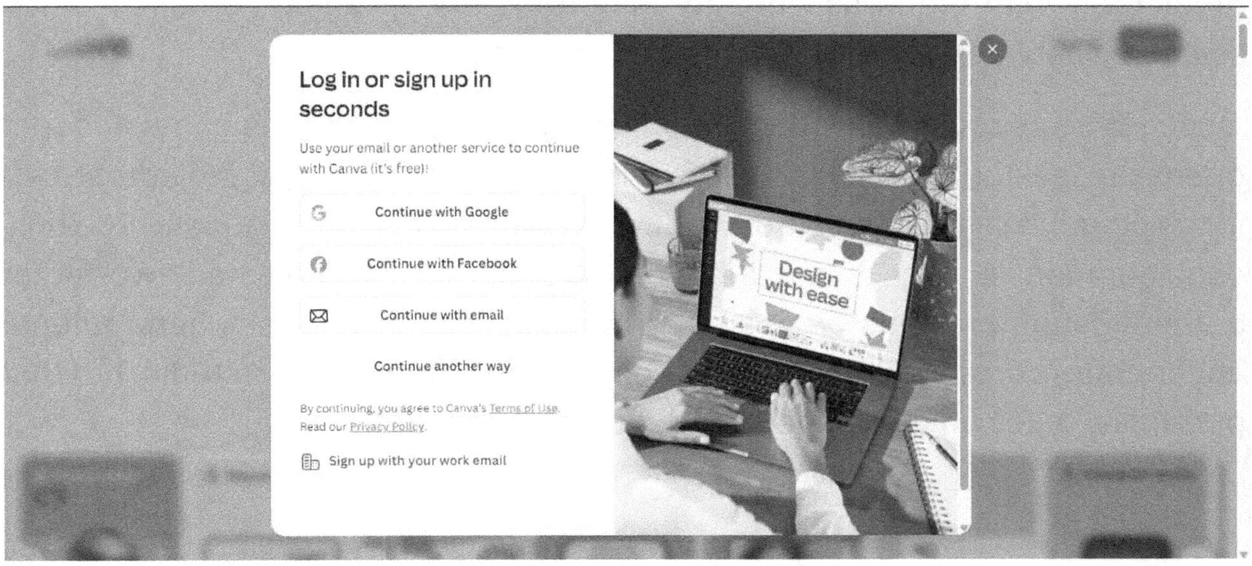

The myth about Canva is that it needs no introduction. Its clean layout and drag-and-drop design suggest instant understanding. Yet beneath that simplicity lies a dense, organized system of features that can either streamline or slow you down depending on how well you navigate it. Knowing where Canva keeps its tools—and why they're arranged that way—transforms casual use into efficient design. What looks like a minimalist workspace is, in truth, a layered hub built for speed, collaboration, and creativity.

Signing Up and Logging In

Creating an account in Canva takes less than a minute, but the choices made at signup shape how the tool functions later. The process starts by visiting Canva's homepage and choosing between a free or paid account. The free plan gives access to thousands of templates, core editing tools, and cloud storage. The paid plans expand those options—adding brand kits, premium templates, and collaboration features—but the base platform remains powerful on its own.

Canva allows logins through Google, Facebook, Apple, or direct email signup. Each has its benefits, but professionals often prefer email registration. It separates work from personal accounts and simplifies permission management across teams. Email-based accounts also integrate more predictably with brand assets and shared folders, avoiding confusion when switching between personal and business projects.

Once registered, Canva works seamlessly across devices. The same account opens on desktop browsers, tablets, and smartphones, with all projects stored in the cloud. Logging in on different devices syncs edits automatically. The only consideration is access security—using strong passwords and two-factor authentication prevents accidental sharing or loss of control when multiple collaborators are involved. Canva's mobility makes it a portable studio, but that portability relies on disciplined account management.

Navigating the Canva Interface

The Home Screen

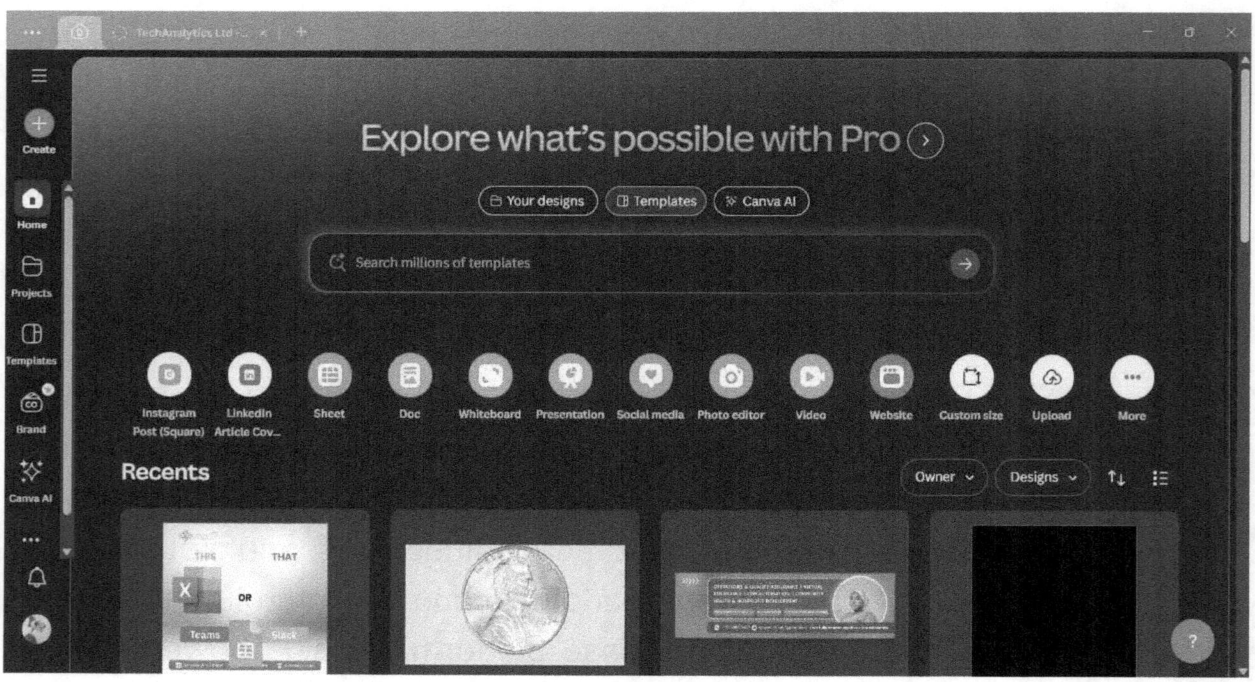

The first thing visible after login is Canva's home screen, a dashboard that organizes everything by purpose. Across the top sits the navigation bar; below it, sections for recent designs, suggested templates, and categorized project types. Each category—Presentations, Posters, Instagram Posts, Logos—represents a preset canvas size with templates designed for that format. Choosing the right type at the start saves resizing work later and ensures designs export correctly.

At the center of this screen, a search bar ties everything together. Typing "menu," "business card," or "wedding invitation" surfaces templates, graphics, and related layouts in seconds. Search doesn't just look for titles; it indexes design categories and keywords, which makes it surprisingly effective when exploring themes like "modern presentation" or "minimal flyer." Those who rely solely on browsing end up spending longer finding what they need.

On the left, the sidebar provides quick access to Projects, Brand, and Trash folders, as well as shared team spaces. It acts like a file directory, keeping personal and collaborative work distinct. The home screen's clean design hides a lot of logic: Canva arranges options around intent—create, manage, collaborate—so designers spend less time navigating and more time creating.

The Sidebar and Top Menu

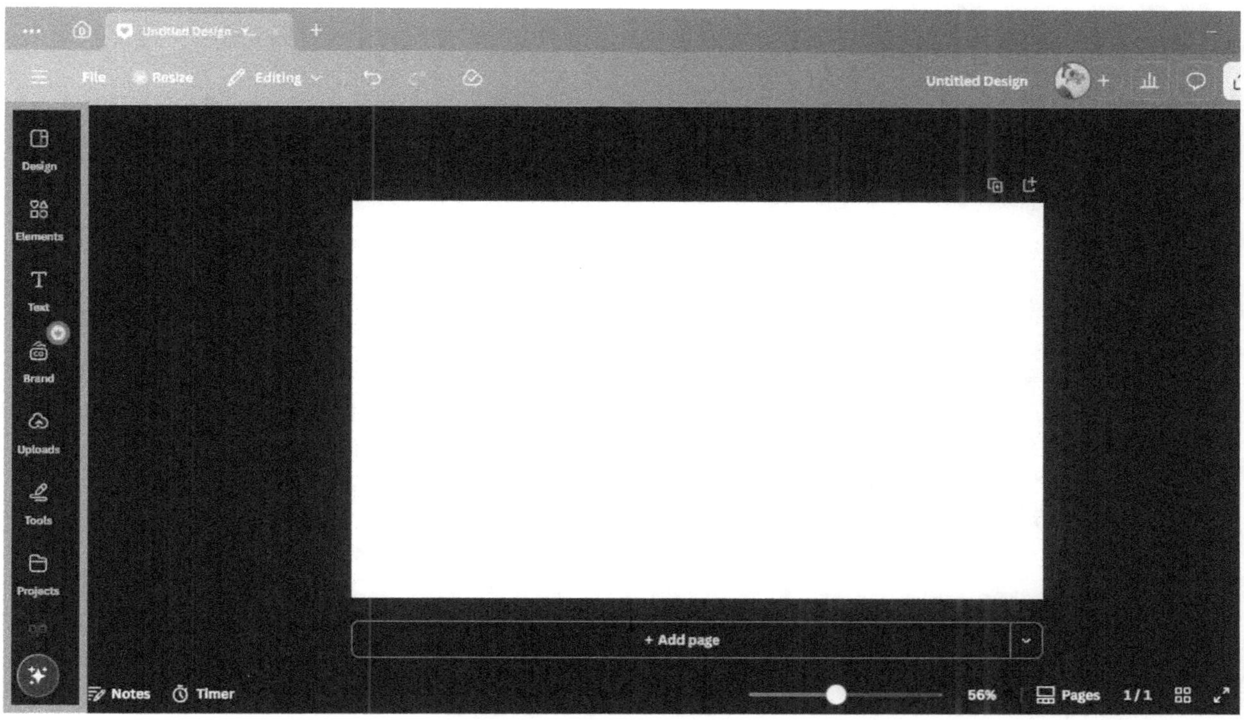

The left sidebar is Canva's control center. "Templates" opens predesigned layouts. "Elements" houses shapes, icons, and illustrations. "Uploads" stores images, videos, and audio imported from your device. "Text," "Photos," and "Audio" provide quick access to Canva's vast media libraries. This separation may seem obvious, but it supports faster recall—templates serve as starting points, while uploads and elements customize those bases.

Above the canvas, the top menu provides global functions. Here live project titles, sharing options, version history, and export controls. It also links to brand kits (in paid plans) and team folders. The top-right corner houses the share button, which connects designs directly to collaborators or publishing channels. Understanding this structure helps explain Canva's philosophy: the left side builds; the top manages. One handles content, the other controls the workflow.

The account menu—found by clicking the profile image—manages personal settings, subscription details, and notifications. It's also where to switch between teams or organizations. Many overlook it, but keeping an eye on account settings ensures access stays organized, especially for those working across multiple projects or clients.

Understanding the Main Workspace

The Canvas Area

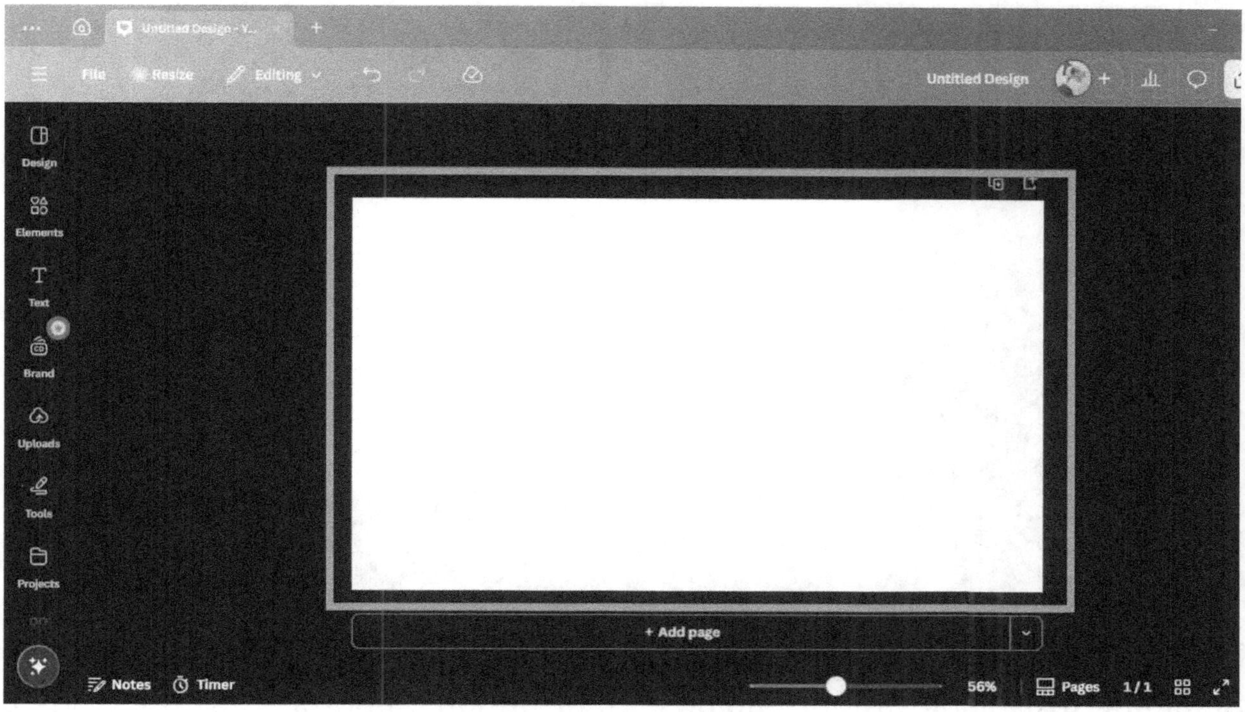

Once a design is opened, the main workspace takes over. The center canvas acts as the creative surface. It's interactive, meaning users can zoom in and out with shortcuts or touch gestures and drag to pan across larger designs. The boundaries of the canvas reflect the chosen format—an Instagram post square, a presentation slide rectangle, or a custom-sized document. Everything visible inside that frame is what exports.

Around the canvas, panels slide in and out depending on what's selected. For example, choosing a photo brings up adjustment tools; selecting text reveals font and alignment controls. These dynamic panels keep the interface uncluttered while offering depth when needed.

For precision work, Canva supports rulers and guides, often enabled through the "View" menu. They help align elements and maintain spacing consistency, especially important in multi-page layouts or branded materials. The behavior mirrors professional design tools but feels more approachable.

The Toolbar and Properties Panel

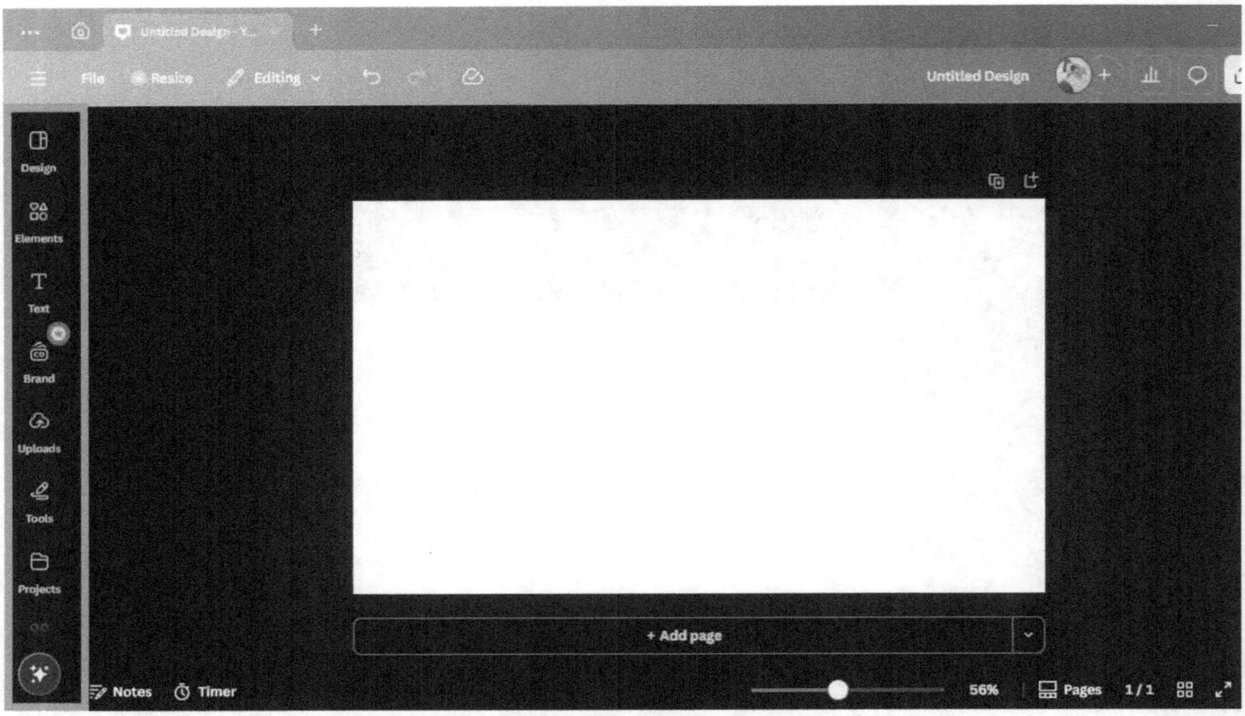

The toolbar above the canvas changes constantly based on what's active. Selecting text displays font choices, color options, and effects. Choosing a photo opens filters, crop tools, and transparency settings. This context-based behavior keeps tools relevant and avoids overwhelming the screen. It also reinforces Canva's learning curve—users gradually discover new functions as their projects evolve.

The properties panel often appears as a floating bar or side tab. It lets designers fine-tune positioning, adjust layering, and tweak details without leaving the workspace. Undo and redo icons sit at the top-left corner, and Canva's version history quietly tracks progress in the background. This feature allows rolling back to earlier edits, an overlooked but essential safeguard during complex projects.

The Pages Panel

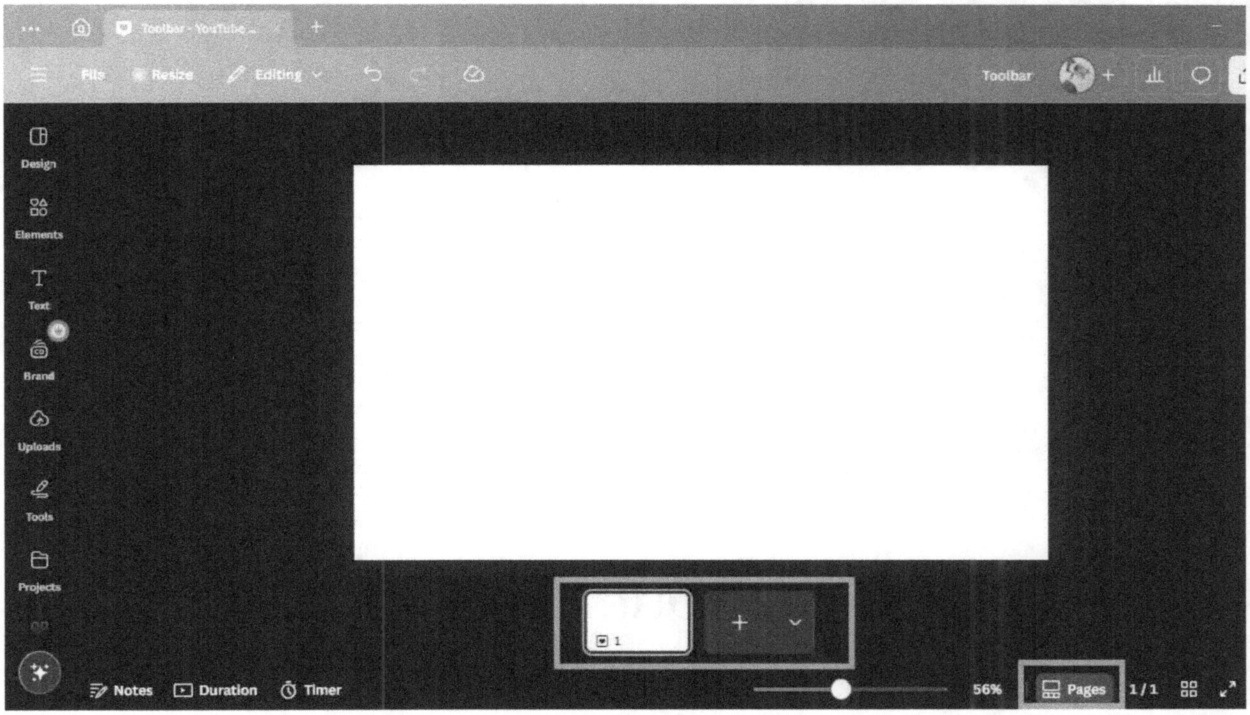

At the bottom of the workspace, thumbnails represent individual pages within a document. Canva treats each page as a slide in a sequence, perfect for presentations, reports, or multi-step visuals. Pages can be duplicated, reordered, or hidden with simple drag actions.

Knowing when to use multiple pages versus separate files depends on purpose. Multi-page designs work best when all visuals share a consistent style—like a pitch deck or brochure. Separate files suit unrelated projects or when collaborating with different teams. Understanding this distinction keeps file organization clean and exports efficient.

Becoming comfortable with Canva's workspace takes less time than learning what hides behind its icons. Familiarity builds through curiosity—hovering over tools, experimenting with options, and noticing small prompts that reveal shortcuts. The interface rewards exploration. What begins as a simple drag-and-drop tool gradually reveals a layered environment where knowing the layout turns casual design into professional output.

Chapter 3: Creating Your First Design

Creating Your First Design

A blank canvas can feel like a challenge, even on a platform built to make design accessible. Canva solves that by offering thousands of templates—ready-made foundations that turn hesitation into progress. But the secret isn't just picking one that looks good. It's knowing how to choose a template that fits the message and how to shape it into something original. The template is a guide, not a shortcut. What matters most is how it's used.

Choosing the Right Template

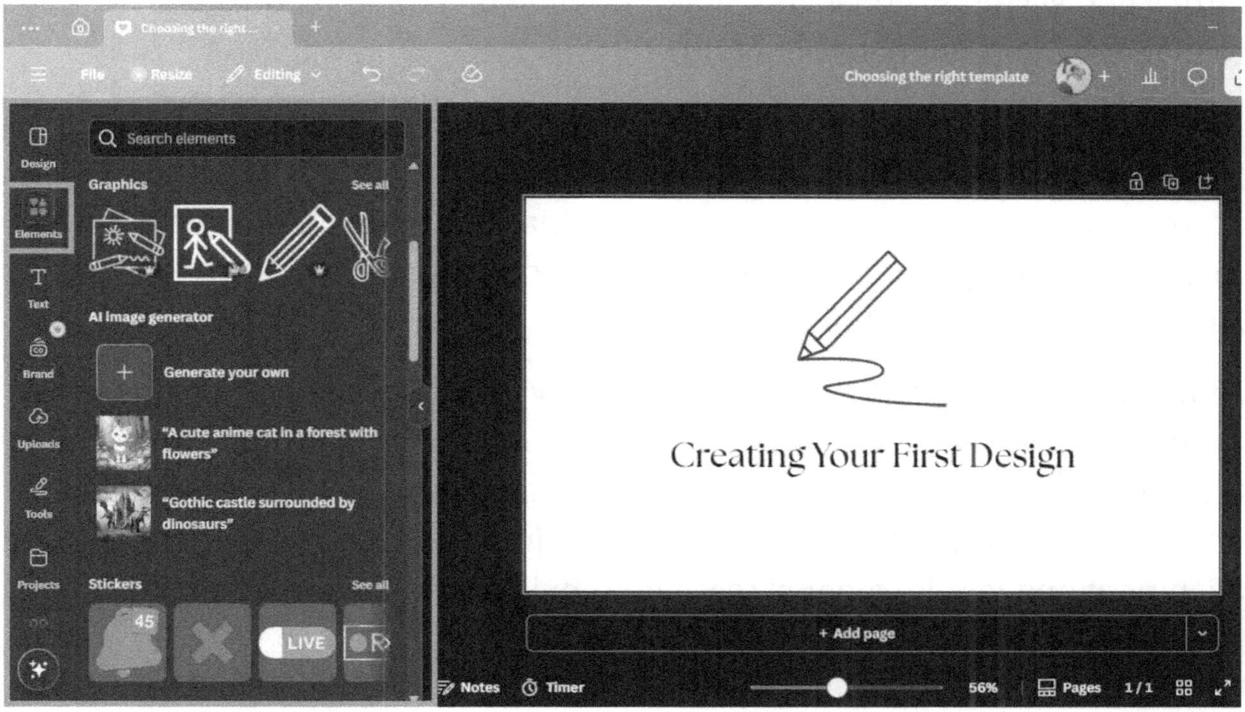

Canva's templates are organized by category, format, and purpose. The homepage separates them into clear sections—social media posts, presentations, marketing materials, and personal designs. Each category narrows into subtypes like "Instagram Story," "Business Presentation," or "Event Poster." This organization matters because every format comes with predefined dimensions, and size determines how a design will display on screens or in print. Choosing the right category from the start means avoiding stretched logos, cropped images, or mismatched proportions later.

Templates influence design quality more than most users realize. A well-structured layout ensures that balance, spacing, and hierarchy already work in harmony. The danger is focusing only on color or style. A minimalist design might look trendy, but if it doesn't support the message—a dense presentation, for instance—it can fail to communicate. Good template selection starts with purpose: What does the design need to achieve? A product flyer must highlight pricing and imagery. A nonprofit poster needs clear calls to action. The layout, not the color palette, drives effectiveness.

Evaluating a template means looking at how it organizes information. Where does the eye go first? Is there room for text, or will adding words clutter the design? Are image placeholders large enough for your visuals? Templates with strong grid systems, consistent margins, and clear contrast between sections tend to adapt better to new content.

Blank templates have their place too. They work best when a design requires full creative freedom or when brand guidelines demand specific layouts. Starting from scratch teaches structure through practice—especially when recreating an idea seen elsewhere. But for most beginners, using a template as a learning tool builds intuition faster.

Dimension choice underpins all of this. Canva provides pre-sized canvases for every format—A4 documents, Instagram squares, YouTube thumbnails. Picking the correct size at the beginning saves time and ensures designs appear correctly wherever they're used. Changing dimensions later can disrupt layout alignment and require manual resizing. The right starting size keeps the project consistent from draft to delivery.

Adding Text, Images, and Shapes

Working with Text

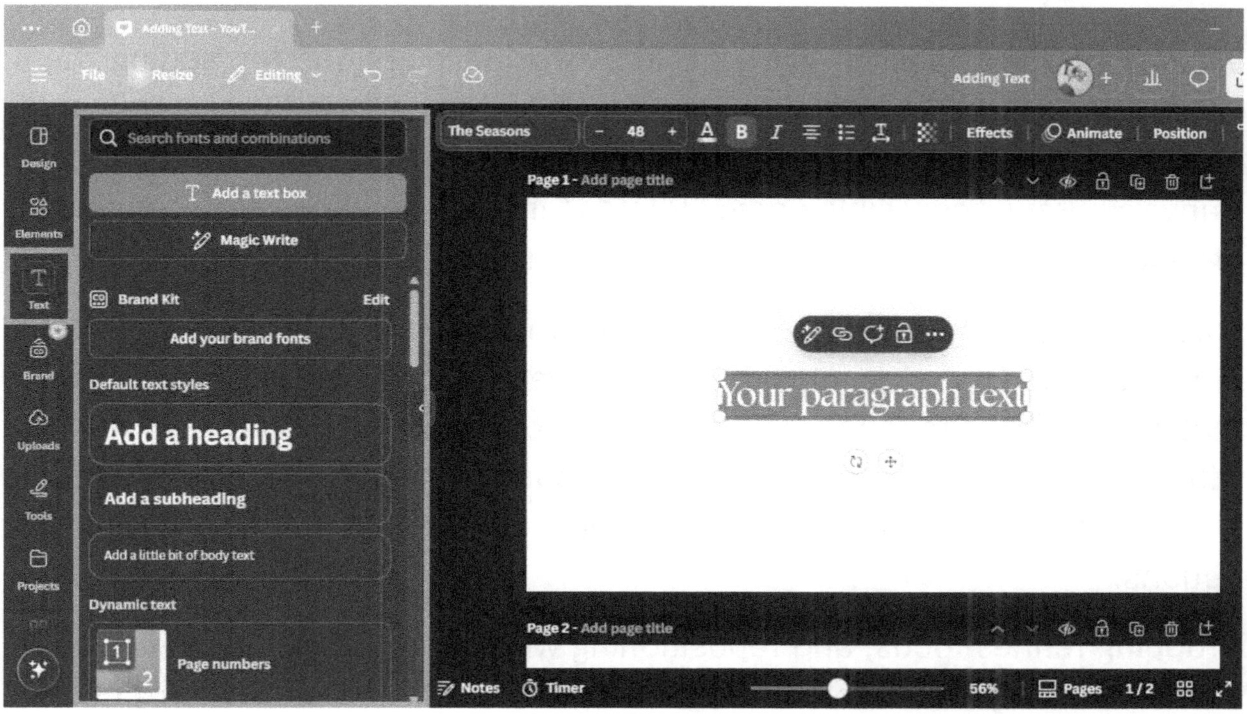

Text brings the message to life, and Canva makes adding it effortless. Clicking "Text" in the sidebar opens options for headings, subheadings, and body text. Adding any of these drops a text box onto the canvas by default. Templates often come preloaded with placeholder text—lorem ipsum or sample slogans—to demonstrate spacing and font pairing. Replacing this with real content instantly transforms the layout into something personal.

Text boxes can be dragged, resized, or rotated by using the bounding handles. Canva's alignment guides help keep everything centered or evenly spaced. Formatting controls appear above the canvas whenever text is selected, offering adjustments for font, color, alignment, and spacing. These tools don't just style words—they define hierarchy. Larger, bolder fonts guide attention; smaller, lighter ones provide supporting context.

Text exists as layers, meaning each box interacts with other design elements. Bringing a photo forward might obscure text unless its layer order is adjusted. Understanding this stacking behavior—moving elements forward or backward—keeps layouts organized and legible. Even simple designs benefit from clean layer management.

Inserting Images

Visuals ground a design. Canva offers two main options for adding them: uploading personal images or selecting from its built-in library. Uploading allows custom photos, product shots, or branded visuals to be stored for reuse. Canva's library, accessible under "Photos," includes millions of images, many of which are free or included with Pro accounts.

Placing an image can be as simple as dragging it onto the canvas. When dropped over a template placeholder, Canva automatically fits and crops it to that frame. This feature—called image containment—keeps layouts neat without manual adjustments. For free-floating images, placement is more flexible. They can be resized, rotated, or cropped directly using the toolbar options.

Cropping refines focus, and repositioning within a frame changes emphasis. Canva's editing tools include brightness, contrast, and saturation controls, letting users align image tone with the rest of the design. Understanding image hierarchy helps too: main visuals should anchor the layout, while supporting graphics remain secondary. Cluttered visuals dilute clarity, so restraint is often more effective than decoration.

Adding Shapes and Elements

Shapes and icons do more than decorate—they guide attention and define structure. The "Elements" tab opens a vast library of lines, geometric forms, and illustrations. Unlike photos, these assets are vector-based, meaning they scale cleanly without losing quality.

Shapes enhance a design when they support balance or highlight content. A rectangle behind text can improve readability. A line can separate sections or frame key points. Problems arise when shapes are added without intention—

too many can compete for attention and confuse the layout. The best use of elements creates rhythm without distraction.

Layering becomes crucial here. Each new element sits on its own layer, which determines what appears on top or behind. The “Position” tool in the top bar manages this order. Sending a shape backward might reveal text, while bringing it forward can create emphasis. Recognizing how layers interact ensures every element serves the design rather than fighting for space.

Saving and Organizing Projects

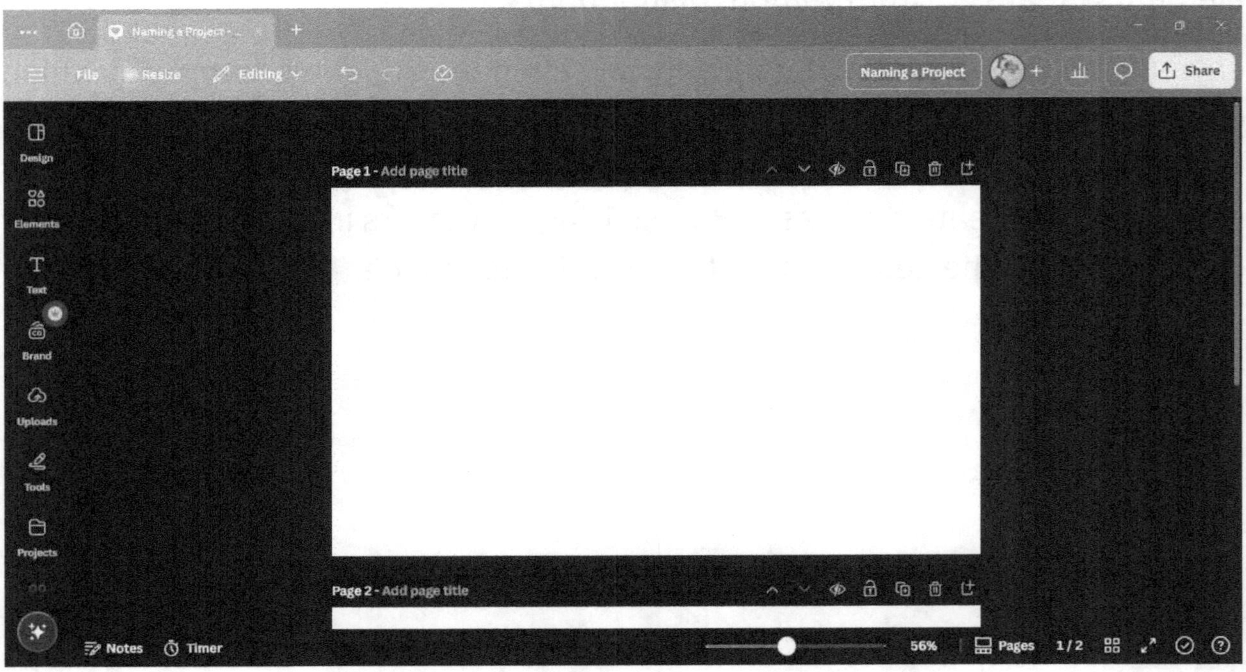

Canva removes the anxiety of forgetting to save. Every edit updates automatically in real time, so progress is never lost. This auto-save feature means users can close a tab mid-project and return later without missing a step. Still, naming projects manually helps avoid confusion—titles like “Q1 Sales Deck” or “Summer Campaign Flyer” make retrieval easier as designs accumulate.

Projects can be sorted into folders for organization. For freelancers, separating client work helps maintain clarity; for teams, folder structure supports collaboration. Folders also store brand assets like logos and templates, creating a centralized library for future designs.

Saving differs from downloading. Saving keeps the editable version in Canva’s cloud, while downloading exports a finished file—JPEG, PNG, PDF, or MP4—ready for sharing or printing. Understanding this difference prevents accidental overwrites and ensures editable backups remain accessible.

Managing Your Projects and Workflow

Canva's cloud storage means every design remains accessible from any device. Past projects appear under "Recent Designs" or in dedicated folders, opening instantly with all layers intact. Duplicating designs is common practice for recurring work—social media posts, reports, or client templates—allowing users to update content without rebuilding layouts.

Old projects can be archived or deleted to reduce clutter. Archiving hides them from the main view but keeps them retrievable later. Deleting removes them permanently, though Canva often confirms before doing so. For long-term users, this cleanup habit keeps workspaces efficient and searchable.

Each design session builds confidence. The first project might feel clumsy, but progress comes through repetition. With each edit, resizing, and experiment, patterns emerge—how layouts balance, how colors interact, how structure directs attention. Canva rewards curiosity. Every attempt teaches something new about how its tools fit together to make ideas visible.

Chapter 4: Working with Text and Typography

Text and Typography

Typography carries more emotional weight than any other design element. The difference between a professional design and an amateur one often comes down to font choices and text treatment, yet these are the aspects beginners overlook most. Fonts shape tone before a single word is read. A handwritten script feels warm and personal, while a clean sans-serif projects structure and confidence. The way text is arranged, spaced, and emphasized determines how easily the message connects. Learning to handle typography in Canva isn't about memorizing settings—it's about understanding how form supports meaning.

Text Editing and Styling

The Text Toolbar

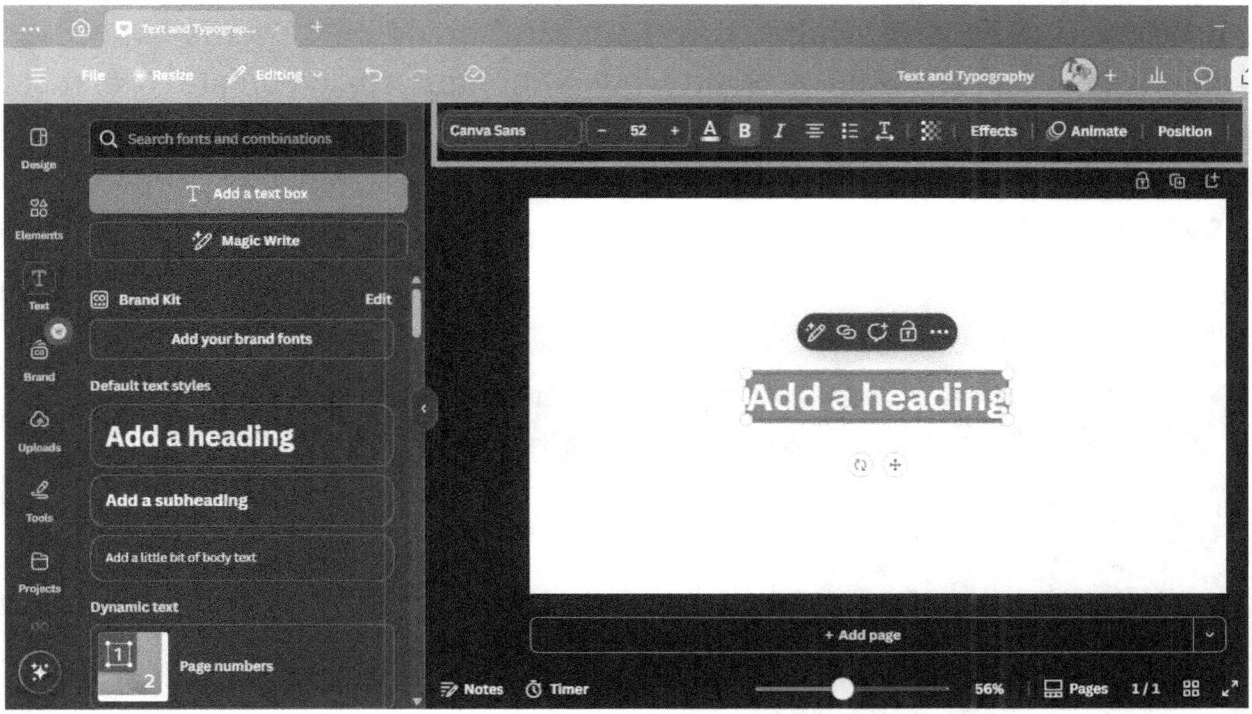

Every text box in Canva unlocks a toolbar packed with options. Once selected, you can change the font, adjust the size, modify colors, and tweak alignment. The toolbar functions as your main control center for text styling. Font selection opens up hundreds of typefaces, organized by categories like serif, sans-serif, script, and display. Each category has its own visual character—serifs bring tradition and authority, sans-serifs feel modern and clean, scripts add personality and warmth.

Sizing controls determine visual hierarchy. Large fonts grab attention, while smaller ones build supporting detail. Color changes are straightforward, but effective use depends on contrast. A pale yellow headline might vanish on a white background, while black text over deep blue can strain the eyes. The key is balance—enough contrast for readability without losing harmony with the overall palette.

Alignment options—left, center, right, and justified—define structure. Left-aligned text feels natural for most readers; centered alignment suits short, symmetrical phrases; right-aligned layouts can look modern but are harder to scan in longer passages. Canva also offers text effects like shadows, outlines, and glow. Used sparingly, they can make titles stand out. Overuse, however, often signals inexperience. Subtle adjustments usually create the most polished look.

Text Hierarchy

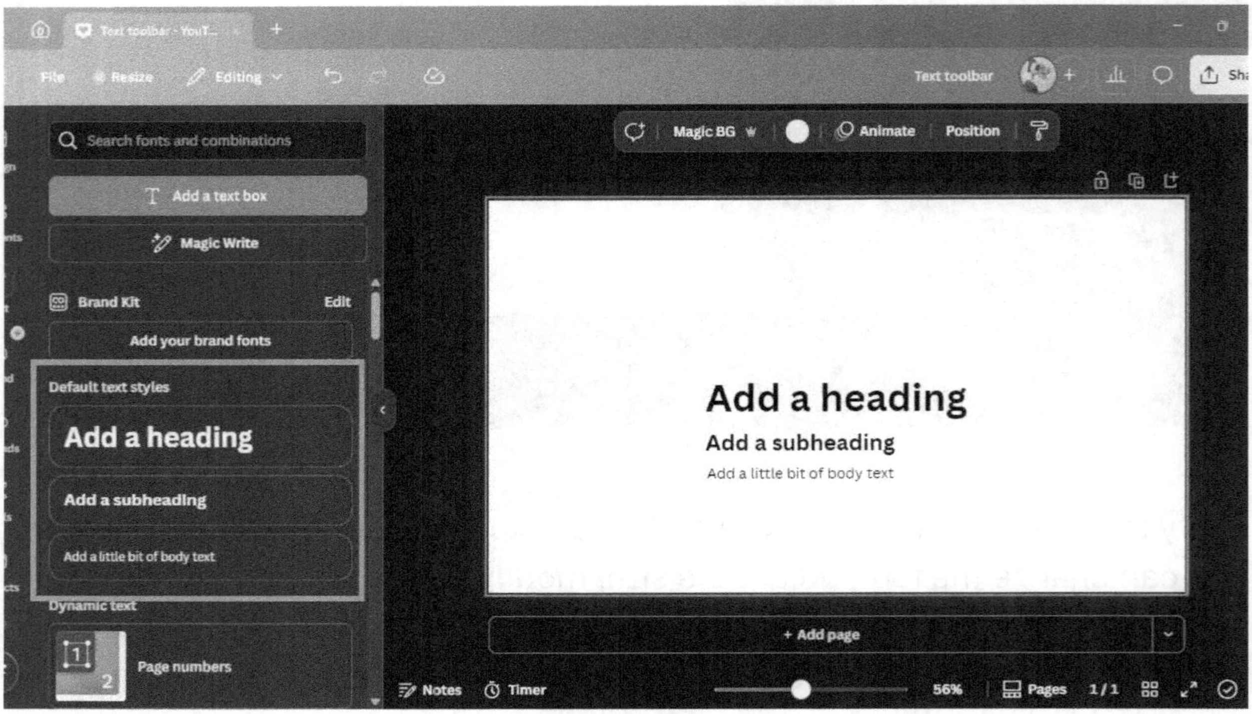

Hierarchy helps the eye navigate a design. Every viewer subconsciously looks for cues about what to read first. Clear differences between heading, subheading, and body text guide that flow. Headings should be largest and boldest, subheadings smaller but still prominent, and body text simple and readable.

Size and weight differences are the easiest way to build hierarchy, but color and spacing also play a role. A headline in a dark tone followed by lighter body text keeps focus where it belongs. Consistent hierarchy across multiple pages or slides creates cohesion. When the same type of text looks identical everywhere, readers immediately recognize its role.

Readability matters most. Fancy fonts lose their appeal if they're hard to decipher. Strong hierarchy is not about decoration—it's about clarity. A viewer should be able to glance once and understand what matters.

Principles of Font Pairing

Using more than one font can strengthen a design, but poor combinations can ruin it. The best pairings build contrast without chaos. Serif and sans-serif pairings are classics for a reason. The serif font provides structure, while the sans-serif keeps the design fresh. Decorative fonts, like hand-lettered or display styles, should appear in moderation—often just for titles or emphasis.

Contrast is key. Two fonts that look too similar compete rather than complement. A bold headline font paired with a light, clean body font feels intentional and balanced. Canva's interface makes experimentation easy, but restraint is important. Two typefaces—three at most—usually suffice.

Fonts carry personality. A geometric sans-serif might communicate technology or minimalism. A round, bubbly typeface feels playful. Matching font tone to content builds emotional consistency. An event flyer for a law firm shouldn't look like a children's party invite.

Font weight variations—regular, medium, bold, or light—can create hierarchy without switching typefaces. This maintains harmony while adding structure. Canva offers pre-designed font pairings that work well as starting points, but it's worth testing adjustments. Sometimes, changing scale or spacing improves balance more than swapping fonts entirely.

Choosing Fonts for Different Purposes

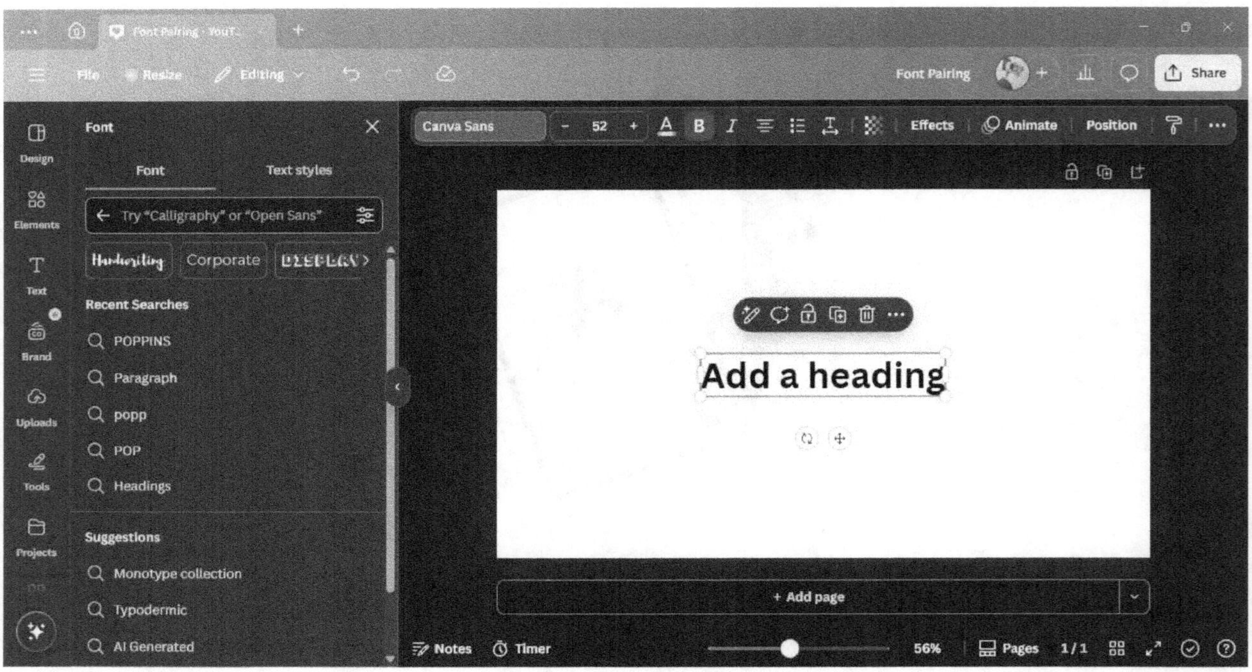

Different projects demand different voices. A business presentation calls for clarity and professionalism, while a fashion lookbook thrives on style and flair. Corporate communications often use stable sans-serifs like Open Sans or Helvetica Neue because they're neutral and readable. Creative fields favor expressive fonts—something with personality but still legible.

Readability shifts with size. What looks elegant at 60 points might be unreadable at 14. Body text requires fonts designed for continuous reading. Headings can afford flair because they appear briefly and in larger sizes. Cultural context also matters. Certain scripts carry national or emotional associations—Old English feels historical, while brush lettering feels contemporary.

Trends come and go, but timeless fonts like Lora, Montserrat, and Roboto stay relevant because they're adaptable. Consider the audience too. Younger viewers may respond to playful, modern fonts; older audiences often prefer clarity over style. The best designs meet users where they are—visually and emotionally.

Adjusting Typography for Readability and Impact

Letter Spacing and Line Height

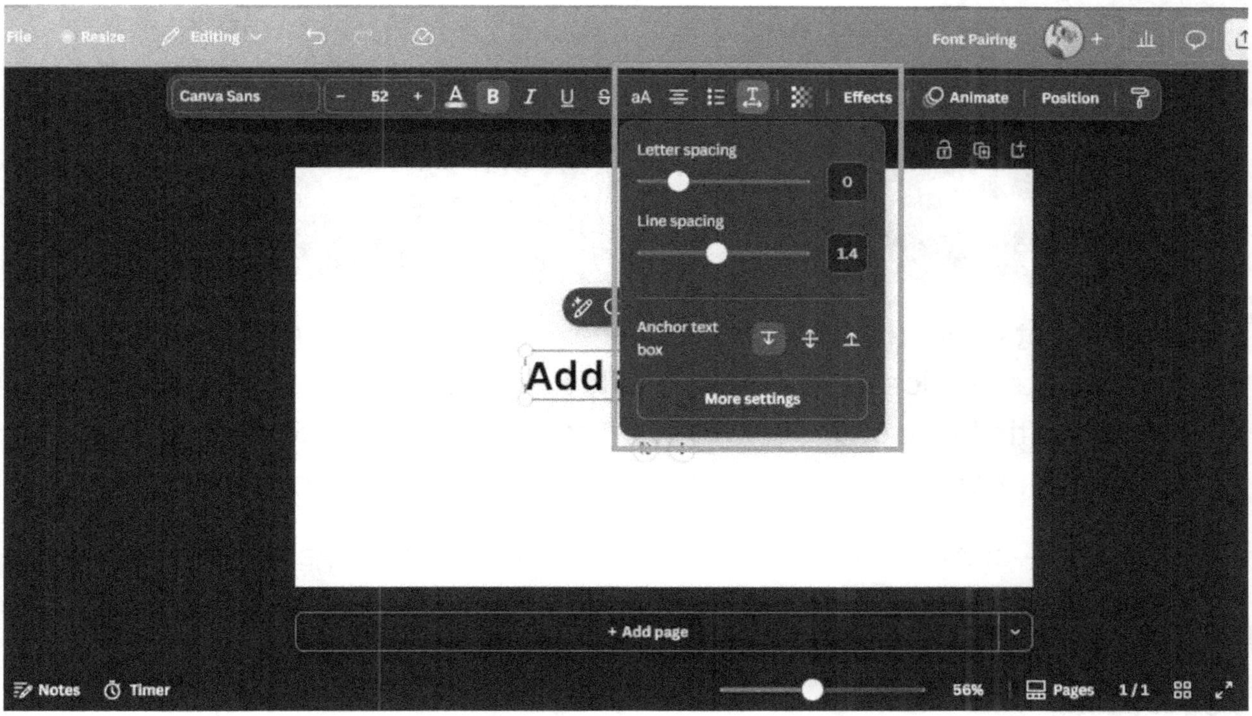

Small spacing tweaks can change how a design feels. Kerning adjusts space between specific letters, while tracking affects spacing across an entire word or line. Tight spacing can make text feel bold and unified, but it risks legibility in long lines. Loose spacing improves readability and can create an airy, open feel.

Line height—the space between lines of text—also shapes readability. Too little, and words blur together; too much, and the text looks disjointed. Canva's sliders make this adjustment simple. For body text, slightly generous spacing helps scanning, especially on screens.

Text Alignment and Justification

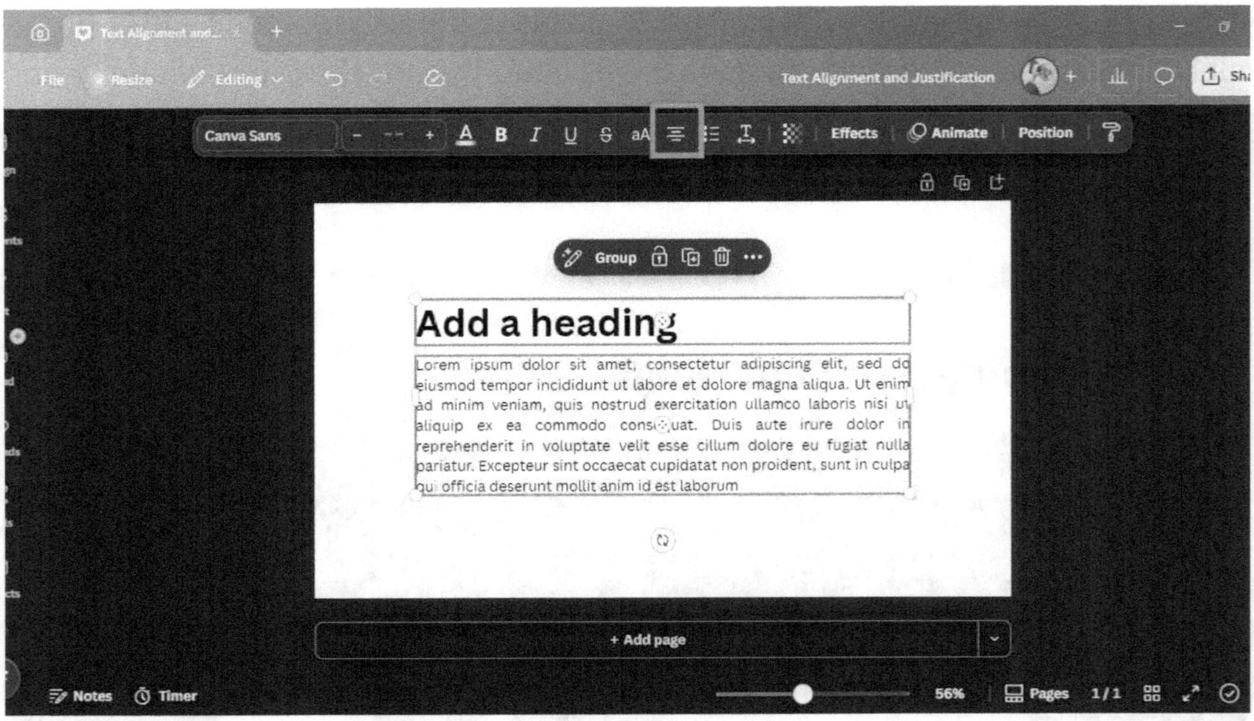

Alignment sets the rhythm of a page. Left alignment creates predictable starting points, which helps reading flow. Centered alignment feels more formal or poetic but works best for short text blocks like quotes or invitations. Right alignment adds visual tension and is often used in minimal designs.

Justified text—common in newspapers—creates clean edges on both sides but can introduce awkward gaps in short passages. Canva's ragged edges are intentional; they keep spacing natural. The goal isn't mechanical neatness—it's visual ease.

Typography mastery doesn't come overnight. It develops through small, conscious choices: cleaner fonts, better spacing, smarter pairings. Even one improvement—a tighter headline, a more readable body font—lifts an entire design. With time, you'll start to see what once felt invisible: the quiet power of type guiding every glance and emotion in your work.

Chapter 5: Images, Photos, and Visual Elements

Images, Photos, and Visual Elements

Images anchor designs emotionally before viewers read a single word. A powerful photo can set tone, context, and credibility all at once. Canva's massive library of stock photos makes access easy, but true design skill lies in knowing which image strengthens the story and how to treat it so it feels intentional rather than generic. Photos aren't decoration—they're part of communication. A well-chosen, well-edited image can turn an average layout into something that feels alive.

Working with Photo Filters and Effects

The Photo Editor Panel

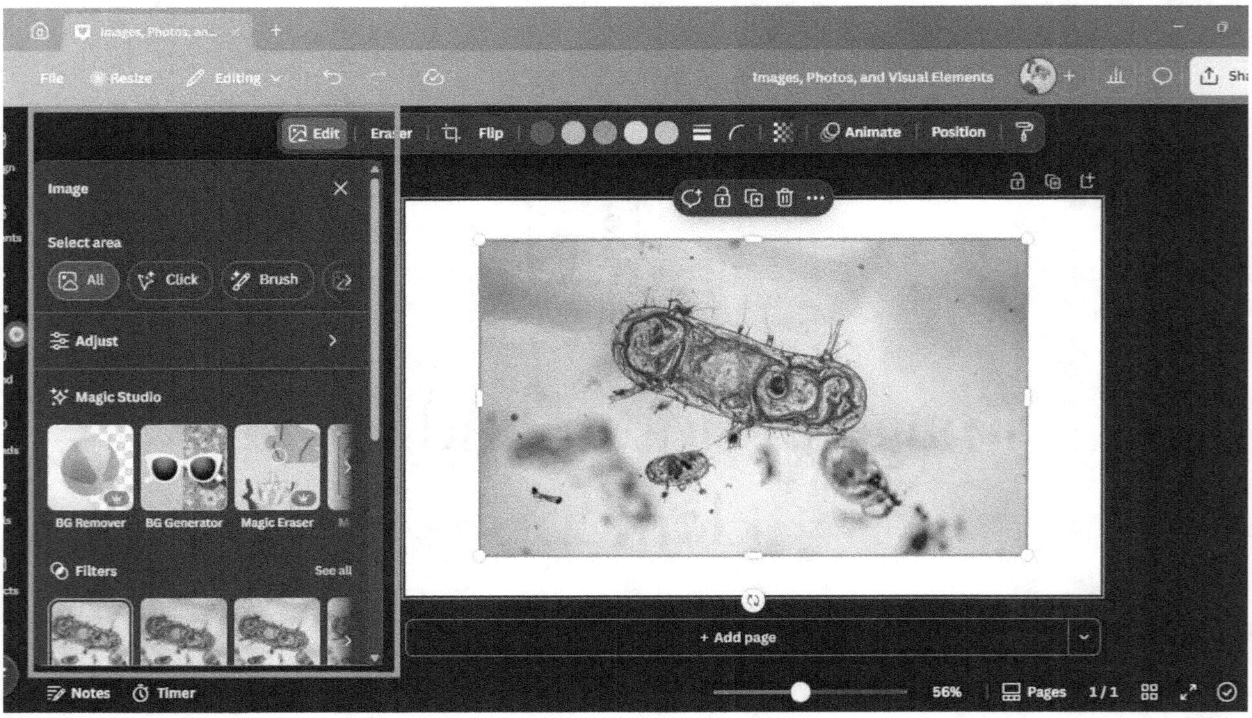

Canva's built-in photo editor is straightforward but surprisingly capable. Select an image, and the top toolbar changes to reveal adjustment tools—brightness, contrast, saturation, blur, and more. The "Edit Photo" button opens a panel where you can fine-tune exposure or apply filters directly. These tools let you shape a photo's mood without ever leaving Canva.

Brightness controls overall light levels; contrast deepens shadows and defines edges; saturation boosts or softens colors. Small changes often make a big difference. Pushing sliders too far usually results in an unnatural look, especially with skin tones or product photos.

Filters offer one-click transformations, but their real value lies in restraint. A filter can unify multiple images in a single design or reinforce a visual style across brand materials. The mistake many beginners make is treating filters like decoration rather than calibration. Subtle filters enhance realism and cohesion. Heavy ones, especially those that distort color or texture, can make a design feel dated or inconsistent.

Color Adjustments

Color defines mood. Canva's tinting and overlay tools help images blend with your design palette. Applying a semi-transparent color block—often a brand color—creates harmony across diverse images. Warm tones like orange and gold add energy; cool tones like blue and gray calm the mood.

Temperature adjustments also influence emotional impact. Cooler photos feel modern and distant; warmer photos feel familiar and human. Matching photo tones with the broader color scheme keeps the composition cohesive. Saturation, meanwhile, determines how bold the visual feels. Bright, saturated images attract attention but can overwhelm text-heavy layouts. Muted tones offer sophistication and keep focus on content. Balance vibrancy with clarity—too much of either breaks flow.

Blur and Focus Effects

Depth adds realism, and Canva simulates it through blur and vignette effects. Background blur mimics shallow depth of field, drawing attention to the main subject. It's especially useful when combining product shots or portraits with text overlays.

Vignettes—subtle darkening around edges—guide the viewer's eyes toward the center. Used sparingly, they create a cinematic feel. Overused, they look artificial. Effects should feel invisible. If viewers notice the technique before the content, it's gone too far. Every adjustment should serve one goal: directing focus to what matters most.

Image Placement and Cropping

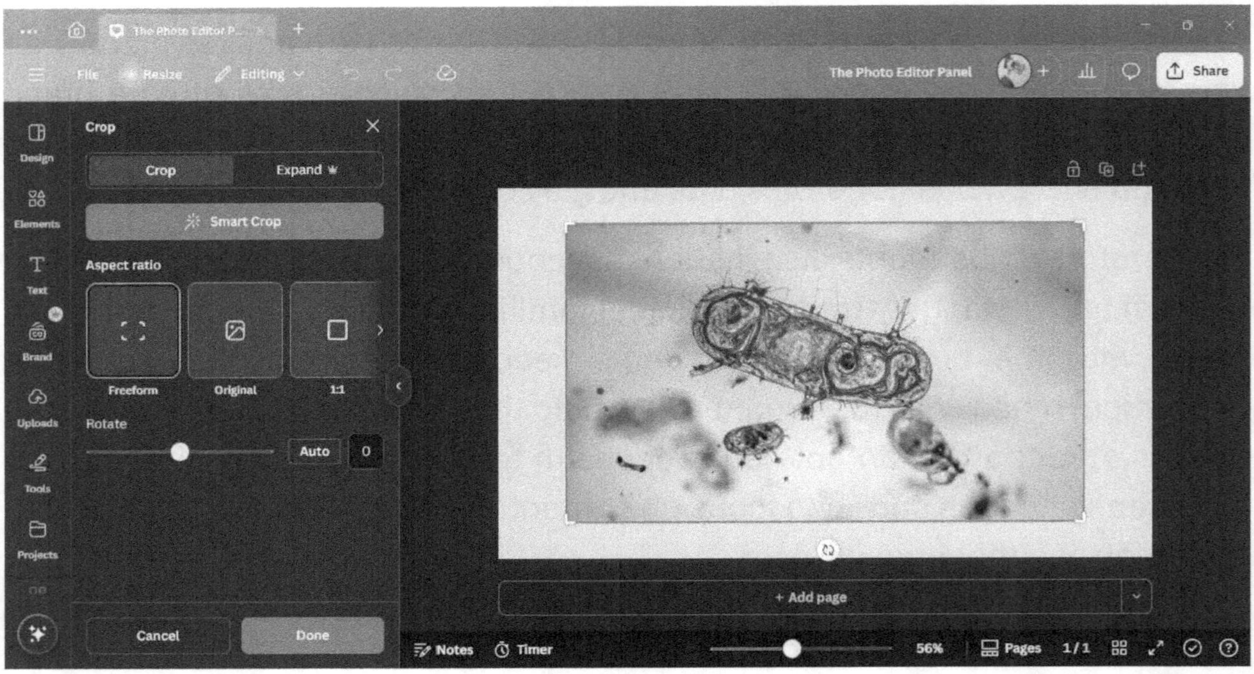

Composition Within Frames

Composition determines how an image communicates. Canva's grid lines help apply the rule of thirds, dividing a frame into nine equal parts. Placing key elements—like faces or products—along those lines naturally creates balance. But this isn't a law. Some photos demand symmetry, while others thrive on asymmetry. What matters is intent.

Cropping affects how the viewer perceives importance. A close crop emphasizes detail or emotion. A wide crop introduces context. Negative space—the area around the subject—provides breathing room for text and icons. Designs overloaded with imagery feel heavy, while those with intentional space look confident and refined.

Orientation also influences tone. Portrait orientation feels personal, great for people or storytelling. Landscape orientation conveys openness and works well for scenes or backgrounds. Choose based on where and how the design will appear—a poster, a phone screen, or a website header.

Cropping for Impact

Cropping is storytelling. Tight crops on a face convey intimacy; wider crops tell environment-driven stories. The same image, reframed differently, can suggest entirely different meanings. A product shot cropped tightly against a neutral background feels focused and premium. The same product placed within a lifestyle scene adds relatability.

For portraits, centered placement can feel formal or static, while off-center placement feels more dynamic and natural. Canva's crop handles make experimentation easy—adjust until the focus feels intentional. Keep aspect ratio in mind, especially for social media. A design meant for Instagram square posts won't translate cleanly to a widescreen layout. Start with the correct dimensions, then crop strategically within them to maintain clarity and composition.

Layering Images with Other Elements

Images rarely stand alone. They interact with text, icons, and shapes. Overlaying text on photos demands careful attention to contrast. Dark text belongs on light areas; light text on dark areas. If the image doesn't offer a natural text-safe zone, add a semi-transparent color overlay or a shape block. This preserves readability without losing the image's visual role.

Transparency adjustments help blend layers smoothly. Lowering opacity can soften photos used as backgrounds, ensuring text remains legible. Overlays also unify multiple design elements into one cohesive look. Layering is about balance—each element should reinforce the message, not compete for attention.

Photo Enhancement Techniques

Lighting Corrections

Lighting determines realism. Many stock photos look great out of the box, but user-uploaded images often need adjustment. Canva's exposure tools can recover slightly underexposed or overexposed areas. Increasing brightness without washing out highlights, or deepening shadows slightly, restores dimension.

The shadow and highlight sliders help correct imbalance: lifting shadows can reveal hidden detail; toning down highlights prevents glare. Overdoing either flattens depth. The goal is to mimic natural lighting conditions, not to make the image “pop” at all costs.

Sometimes, it’s better to replace a photo than to fix it. Blurry, low-resolution, or poorly lit images can rarely be saved through editing. Knowing when to let go saves time and strengthens the final design.

Sharpness and Clarity

Sharpness enhances detail, but too much creates noise and hard edges. Canva’s sharpen tool should be used gently, especially with portraits—over-sharpened faces look unnatural. Clarity adds midtone contrast, boosting texture and perceived depth. It’s ideal for landscapes or product photos where crispness adds realism.

The balance between sharpness and softness shapes tone. High clarity feels bold and tactile; low clarity feels dreamy or nostalgic. Think about what emotion the image should convey before adjusting.

Background Removal Basics

Canva’s Background Remover, available in the Pro version, isolates subjects with one click. It’s invaluable for creating clean product mockups, profile images, and collages. The tool automatically detects edges, removing unwanted backgrounds instantly.

After removal, zoom in to inspect edges. Fuzzy or uneven cutouts break realism. The “Erase” and “Restore” brushes refine edges manually. Clean cutouts ensure the subject blends naturally with new backgrounds. Transparent PNG downloads preserve flexibility for later use.

Background removal works best for subjects with clear outlines and contrast. Complex, detailed backgrounds or hair textures may need fine-tuning. The best cutouts feel seamless, not artificial.

Photo treatment should never steal attention. The viewer should feel the result, not see the process. Editing is invisible craftsmanship—balancing tone, clarity, and placement so that the image supports the message effortlessly. In Canva, the difference between a beginner and a thoughtful designer isn't access to features—it's knowing when to stop.

Chapter 6: Shapes, Icons, and Illustrations

Shapes seem deceptively simple—circles, squares, lines. Yet these basic elements form the foundation of nearly every design. They create structure, guide attention, and organize content in ways that text and photos alone cannot. Icons and illustrations extend that logic, translating complex ideas into visuals that are instantly understood. In Canva, these components are more than decoration—they're the language of composition.

Using Elements, Backgrounds, and Grids

The Elements Library

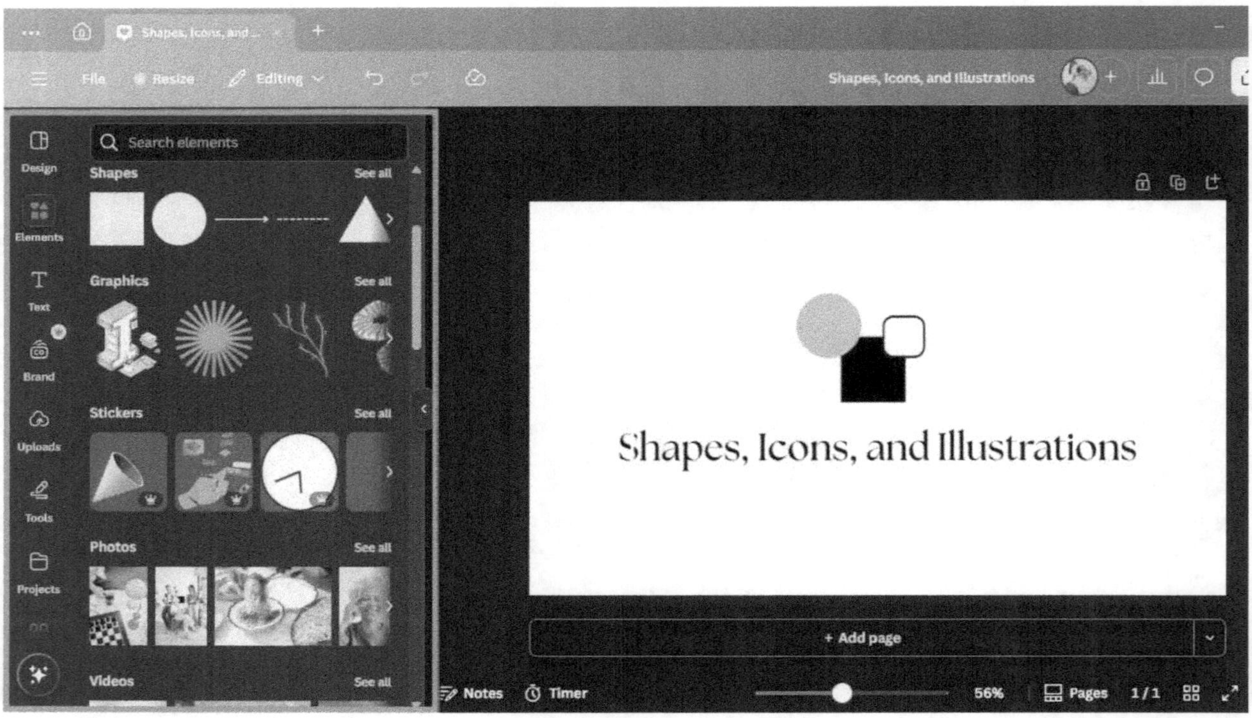

The Elements panel is Canva's toolbox for structure and detail. It houses shapes, lines, graphics, stickers, charts, and frames. Each category serves a different function, but they share one goal: to make layouts clear and expressive. Elements appear under distinct sections, and Canva's search bar helps filter them by theme, color, or style. Searching "minimal line icon," for example, narrows results more effectively than a single keyword like "icon."

Static shapes, such as circles and rectangles, can be resized and recolored freely. Customizable graphics, on the other hand, often include editable color sections or multiple layers. Some respond to brand colors automatically, adjusting hues when a palette is applied. Free and paid elements are marked clearly—premium ones feature a crown icon. This distinction matters when working in shared designs, since using paid elements without a Pro account leaves a watermark that affects the final export.

The key to mastering the Elements library isn't finding the perfect graphic—it's understanding how to combine simple ones purposefully. A clean layout built with shapes and lines often communicates more clearly than a crowded one filled with unrelated visuals.

Basic Shapes

Shapes are the building blocks of visual logic. A rectangle becomes a banner, a circle becomes a highlight, and a triangle suggests direction. The way these shapes interact defines a design's rhythm. Fill shapes establish visual mass, while outlined shapes create contrast and structure. Adjusting transparency softens edges and adds depth without distraction.

Color transforms how shapes behave. A bold red rectangle commands attention; a pale gray one recedes into the background. Size establishes hierarchy—large shapes frame key content, small ones balance composition. Rotation changes energy: horizontal feels stable, diagonal adds movement. Even subtle angles alter how viewers read the design's flow.

Used sparingly, shapes help anchor content. Overused, they clutter space and dilute focus. The strength of basic forms lies in how intentionally they're placed, not how many appear.

Lines and Dividers

Lines are visual separators that create order. They guide the eye, divide sections, and subtly control pacing. A thin horizontal line can separate a header from body text without feeling heavy. Vertical lines create tension and formality, often used in infographics or business layouts.

Line weight changes the message. Thin lines feel elegant and minimal; thick ones suggest strength and certainty. Dotted or dashed lines add rhythm and movement. Decorative dividers—such as flourishes or illustrated breaks—work when they align with the design's tone. In minimalist layouts, they often distract.

Lines don't just separate—they connect. Aligned properly, they draw attention from one element to another, ensuring the design reads in a logical sequence.

Background Elements

Backgrounds shape atmosphere. Canva allows full-bleed backgrounds that stretch edge-to-edge or contained backgrounds that live within frames or shapes. Both serve different purposes. Full-bleed backgrounds anchor a design in color or texture; contained shapes create focus areas.

Patterns and textures add tactile realism but can compete with text if overused. Text readability always takes priority—busy patterns behind type weaken hierarchy. When using image-based backgrounds, applying a semi-transparent overlay often restores clarity.

Gradients, once dismissed as outdated, have reemerged in modern design. Smooth transitions between two colors add depth and vibrancy. The trick lies in restraint—gradients should complement, not overpower. The best backgrounds sit quietly, supporting the foreground instead of stealing from it.

Working with Icons and Illustrations

Icons and illustrations communicate faster than text. Icons distill ideas into simple, recognizable forms—a phone for contact, a globe for travel. Illustrations, meanwhile, add character and emotion. They can set tone, convey friendliness, or make abstract ideas tangible.

Style consistency is crucial. Mixing flat icons with shaded illustrations breaks visual harmony. Canva's library includes both, but sticking to one aesthetic—

line art, filled icons, or dimensional graphics—keeps a design cohesive. A design built with flat icons throughout feels intentional; one that mixes cartoonish drawings with geometric icons feels uneven.

Size matters. Icons that are too small lose legibility, especially on mobile screens. Oversized icons, however, can feel childish or overpower text. The goal is proportional balance—icons should reinforce hierarchy without dominating it.

Canva allows most icons to be recolored, aligning them with the brand palette. A consistent color system ties disparate elements together, even when sourced from different creators.

Icons clarify meaning when used thoughtfully. A calendar beside a date adds clarity. But repeating obvious information—like placing a phone icon next to a number labeled "Phone"—adds redundancy. The best icons act as visual shortcuts, not echoes of what's already said.

Cultural context also matters. Symbols that feel universal may mean different things elsewhere. A checkmark indicates success in some regions but signals error in others. Awareness of these nuances ensures designs remain inclusive and effective across audiences.

Creating Custom Graphics

Combining Shapes

Canva's simple shapes can be combined to create unique graphics. Two overlapping circles form a Venn diagram. A rectangle and triangle can become a flag. These small compositions turn abstract ideas into structured visuals. Layering shapes creates hierarchy—foreground shapes carry more weight than those behind.

Alignment tools ensure precision. The "Tidy Up" and "Position" options snap elements into balanced arrangements. Grouping shapes once aligned keeps them movable as a single unit, making edits easier later.

Color harmony ties these custom graphics together. Limiting combinations to two or three tones keeps designs clean. Multiple saturated colors quickly become overwhelming. Subtle shade differences can suggest depth without cluttering the visual.

Editing Existing Elements

Canva's pre-made graphics aren't fixed. Many can be customized, recolored, or partially edited. Unlocking grouped illustrations reveals individual components—useful when removing unnecessary parts or isolating a section for reuse.

Color swapping lets designers adjust illustrations to fit brand guidelines. Changing a graphic's accent color from bright blue to muted beige can instantly align it with a more professional palette. Some complex illustrations use gradients or layered tones that resist full recoloring, but even limited tweaks can improve fit.

Sometimes, editing an existing element is more efficient than building one from scratch. Adjusting proportions, removing small details, or recoloring a graphic saves time while maintaining visual coherence.

Shapes and icons are the quiet architects of visual communication. They don't demand attention—they direct it. Together, they provide the scaffolding that text and images rely on. In Canva, mastering these tools isn't about decoration. It's about building structure, clarity, and rhythm so every design feels deliberate, even in its simplest form.

Chapter 7: Color Theory and Application in Design

Color Theory and Application in Design

Color shapes perception before words or layout have a chance. It sets the emotional tone, influences behavior, and determines whether a design feels modern or dated. Mastering color theory isn't about memorizing art school terminology—it's about understanding how visual energy works and how to channel it effectively in Canva.

Basics of Color Theory

The Color Wheel

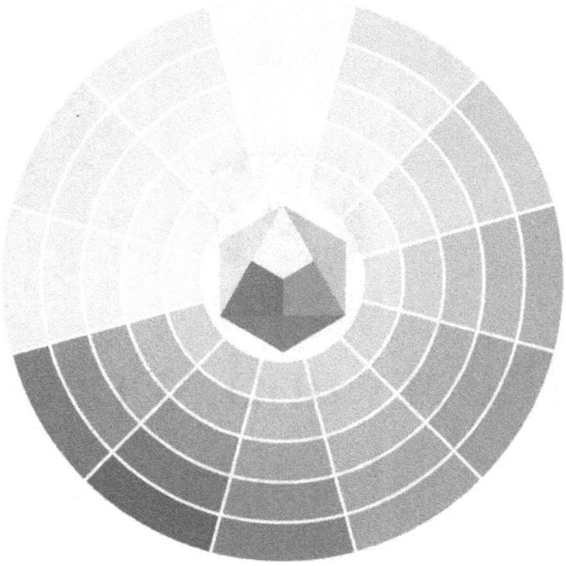

The color wheel is the foundation of visual harmony. It organizes hues into relationships that make sense to the eye. Primary colors—red, blue, and yellow—are the base; all other colors stem from mixing these three. Combine them to get secondary colors: orange, green, and purple. Blend further, and you get tertiary colors like red-orange or blue-green, which soften transitions between strong hues.

Colors are often categorized as warm or cool. Warm tones like red, orange, and yellow feel energetic and immediate. They create urgency, optimism, and warmth. Cool tones—blue, green, and purple—suggest calm, professionalism, and trust. Neither is better; their power lies in intent. A spa ad leaning on blues feels serene, while a fast-food promo using reds and yellows pushes for instant attention.

Every color carries psychological weight.

- **Red**: urgency, energy, appetite. Used in sales, alerts, and call-to-action buttons.

- **Blue**: stability, trust, and calm. Common in finance, tech, and healthcare.
- **Green**: renewal, growth, and nature. Works for sustainability and wellness brands.
- **Yellow**: optimism and creativity—but too much can signal caution or strain the eyes.

Culture also shapes meaning. White signals purity in many Western contexts but mourning in parts of Asia. Understanding your audience ensures color choices land correctly, not awkwardly.

Color Relationships

Colors don't exist in isolation—they gain meaning in combination.

- **Complementary colors** sit opposite each other on the wheel, like blue and orange. The contrast grabs attention but should be balanced carefully to avoid visual tension.
- **Analogous colors**—neighbors on the wheel, like blue, teal, and green—offer harmony. They feel natural and pleasing, often used in gradients or smooth transitions.
- **Triadic schemes** (three colors evenly spaced around the wheel) create dynamic, balanced energy—ideal for playful brands or youth-focused visuals.
- **Monochromatic palettes**, built from one hue with different values, create unity and sophistication. They're perfect for minimal or corporate designs where restraint communicates confidence.

Saturation and Value

Two designs can use the same hue but feel entirely different based on brightness and intensity.

Value describes how light or dark a color appears; **saturation** measures its vividness.

Desaturated palettes—think dusty rose or faded navy—feel modern and professional. Vibrant ones scream energy and youth. Neither is right or wrong; each has its moment.

You can adjust tone with:

- **Tints** (add white) for softness,
- **Shades** (add black) for depth,
- **Tones** (add gray) for neutrality.

A good designer uses these variations to balance excitement with readability.

Applying Color Palettes in Canva

Canva's Color Tools

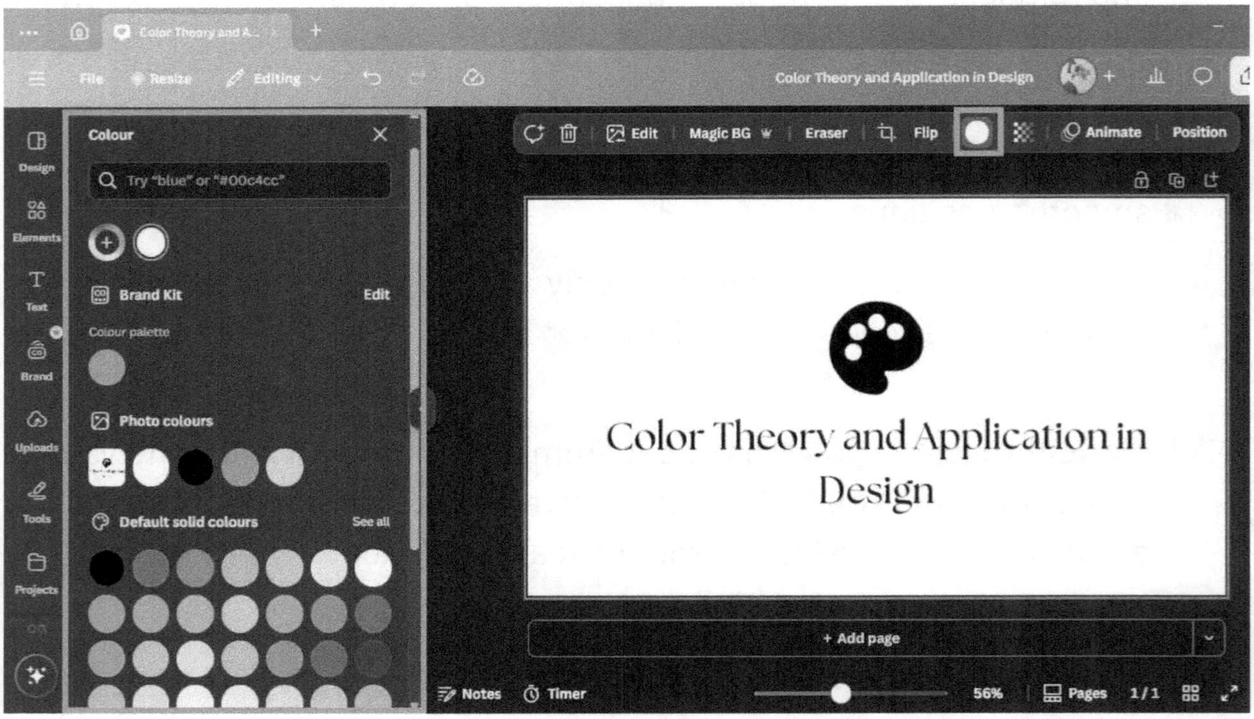

Canva makes color control accessible. The **color picker** lets you choose hues by eye, or precisely through **hex codes** (e.g., #007BFF) and **RGB values.** These codes ensure consistency—vital for brand visuals.

Recent colors appear automatically for reuse, and you can save palettes for specific projects. The **eyedropper tool** extracts colors from images, letting photos dictate your scheme—a quick way to ensure harmony between graphics and backgrounds.

Pre-Made Palettes

Canva also suggests ready-made palettes, often inspired by templates or trending color combinations. These can be a time-saver but should be used thoughtfully. A palette built for a tropical travel poster might clash with a minimalist business ad.

Photo-based palettes, where Canva pulls colors directly from an uploaded image, often yield cohesive, natural results. They're excellent for brand storytelling—matching visuals to photography seamlessly.

Building Custom Palettes

A strong palette starts with a **dominant color**—the anchor that defines the tone. From there, build secondary and accent colors around it. The **60-30-10 rule** helps maintain balance: 60% dominant, 30% secondary, 10% accent. This isn't a strict law, just a useful structure to keep visuals from feeling chaotic.

Limit your palette to **three to five colors**. More than that, and your design risks inconsistency. For multi-page designs—like presentations or social campaigns—carry the same palette throughout. Consistency signals professionalism and strengthens recognition.

Using Colors to Evoke Mood and Message

Matching Color to Purpose

Color choices should serve the message. Corporate industries lean on blues, grays, and muted tones to express reliability. Creative fields—fashion, art, media—embrace bold or experimental hues.

Industries also develop color expectations:

- **Healthcare**: blue or green for calm and trust.
- **Food**: warm tones like red and orange to stimulate appetite.
- **Luxury brands**: black, gold, or deep hues for exclusivity.

Color trends shift with seasons too. Pastels feel fresh in spring; deep jewel tones fit autumn. Younger audiences gravitate toward bright, saturated colors, while mature ones respond to subtlety and depth.

Contrast and Readability

Good design isn't just beautiful—it's functional. High contrast between text and background ensures readability. White text on a pale background or black text over navy can make content frustrating to read.

A quick trick: convert your design to grayscale. If the hierarchy still holds up, the contrast is solid. Accessible color contrast benefits everyone, not just those with visual impairments.

Color Trends and Timelessness

Design trends evolve, and so do color preferences. Current palettes emphasize muted pastels, earthy tones, and minimal contrast—but what's fashionable now might feel dated in a year.

The key is balance. Follow trends in small doses while keeping your core palette stable. Brands with longevity—like Coca-Cola or Apple—stick to consistent colors while adapting how they're applied. Trendy accents can modernize a design, but timeless palettes build trust and recognition.

Color isn't decoration; it's communication. Each hue carries a story, emotion, and purpose. Mastering color theory in Canva isn't about making things "look pretty." It's about designing with intent—where every shade works to send the right signal, to the right audience, at the right moment.

Chapter 8: Layout and Composition Design

Layout and Composition Design

Composition guides the viewer's eyes. It shapes the story before a word is read or a color is processed. Good design composition isn't about decoration—it's about structure and flow. When done right, it feels invisible. When it's off, even a stunning design feels confusing or unbalanced.

Principles of Effective Layout

Visual Hierarchy

Visual hierarchy determines what gets noticed first. It's how you direct attention through deliberate contrast in size, color, and placement. Big elements signal importance; bold colors attract the eye; central or upper placements dominate.

Western viewers naturally follow **Z-patterns** (for simple layouts) or **F-patterns** (for text-heavy designs). In the Z-pattern, the eye moves from top left to top right, diagonally down, then across the bottom—ideal for posters or landing pages. The F-pattern fits articles, where users scan down the left edge for headlines and across short bursts of text.

Establishing a **focal point** anchors attention. Whether it's a headline, product image, or call-to-action button, the focal point gives the viewer direction. Everything else supports it. If every element shouts for attention, the design becomes noisy.

Sometimes breaking hierarchy intentionally—like tilting a single image or using unexpected color—creates impact. Disruption works when there's already a visible structure to break from.

Balance and Symmetry

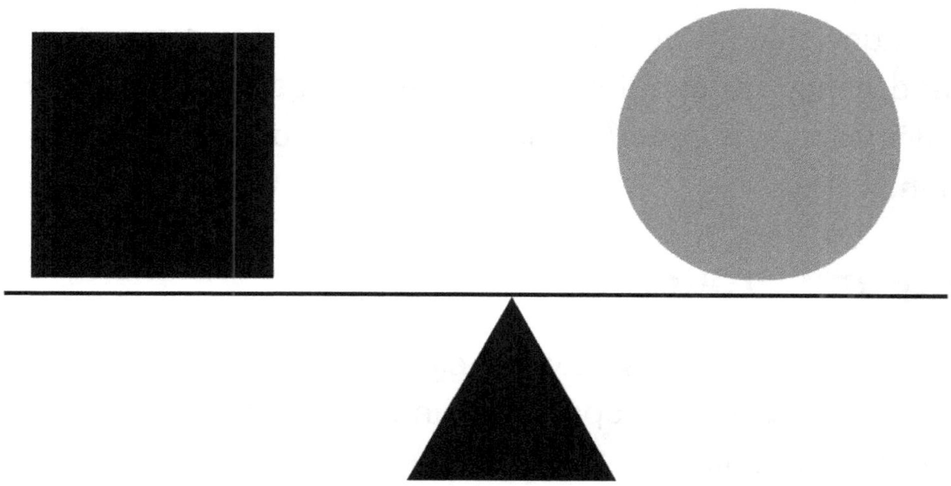

Balance controls how comfortable or dynamic a design feels.

- **Symmetrical balance** mirrors both sides. It's predictable, calm, and formal—great for certificates or business reports.
- **Asymmetrical balance** uses unequal but visually equivalent elements. A large light area can balance a smaller dark one. This approach feels modern and active.

Every object has **visual weight**. Dark tones, bold fonts, and dense textures pull the eye more strongly than light or small ones. The trick is understanding that balance isn't about identical halves—it's about emotional equilibrium.

Designs also have a **physical center** and a **visual center**. They rarely align perfectly. The visual center often sits slightly above the true middle; placing your main subject there creates natural balance.

Radial balance, where elements radiate from a core (like a logo or badge), works best for circular layouts that need central focus.

Whitespace and Breathing Room

Whitespace—often called negative space—isn't empty. It's what lets content breathe. It defines edges, highlights key elements, and sets tone. Crowded layouts feel cheap and stressful. Spacious ones feel confident and high-end.

Beginners often fill every inch, fearing "unused" space. In truth, deliberate emptiness is design control. Whitespace around text improves legibility. Wide margins and generous padding make content feel intentional. In premium branding, whitespace *is* luxury—it signals that the design doesn't have to fight for attention.

Proximity and Grouping

Proximity builds relationships between elements. Items placed close together are perceived as related. Separating unrelated content helps the viewer process information quickly.

For example, a headline, subtext, and icon clustered together read as a single thought. But scatter them apart and they lose unity.

This invisible rule—group what belongs, separate what doesn't—reduces clutter and makes layouts readable. Visual logic replaces guesswork, and users navigate your design without thinking about it.

Using Grids and Alignment Tools

Grid Systems in Canva

Canva's built-in **alignment guides** act as invisible scaffolding. They appear as pink lines when dragging elements, helping you align text, images, and icons with precision.

Objects **snap** to these guides automatically. You can override snapping for fine adjustments, but it's best to use it for alignment consistency.

Column-based layouts are the backbone of professional design. They divide a canvas into predictable zones, maintaining order even when visuals vary.

For photography and banners, the **rule of thirds** grid helps placement. Positioning key elements along one of the grid's vertical or horizontal thirds creates natural harmony—used in everything from magazine covers to social posts.

Alignment Precision

Text alignment carries meaning.

- **Left-aligned text** feels grounded and readable, perfect for paragraphs.
- **Center alignment** creates formality but can look messy when overused.
- **Right alignment** is best for small design accents or symmetry.

Aligning multiple elements to the same invisible line gives structure. Misaligned edges create subconscious tension. Canva's **Position tool** allows pixel-level control, so even small objects line up perfectly.

Center-aligning every object is a beginner trap. Variety—using alignment intentionally—adds rhythm and flow.

Spacing and Distribution

Even spacing between elements separates amateur work from polished design. Canva's **Tidy Up** or distribution options automatically equalize gaps between multiple items, ensuring consistent rhythm.

Horizontal spacing works for rows; vertical spacing organizes stacked sections. Inconsistent spacing breaks flow and makes designs feel sloppy.

But strict uniformity can be dull. Breaking spacing intentionally—adding extra room around a focal element—creates emphasis and focus. The goal is deliberate rhythm, not robotic repetition.

Balancing Visual Elements

Text-to-Image Ratios

Text and imagery compete for dominance. The right balance depends on purpose.

- **Text-heavy designs** (infographics, guides) prioritize clarity. Use imagery sparingly to reinforce, not distract.
- **Image-driven layouts** (ads, covers) communicate emotion fast. Text should support, not overwhelm.

Too many focal points split attention; the viewer doesn't know where to look. Whitespace acts as the separator, ensuring hierarchy remains clear.

Layering for Depth

Designs are two-dimensional, but layering creates the illusion of depth. Think of three levels:

- **Background** (texture, color, or image),
- **Midground** (main visuals),
- **Foreground** (text or key icons).

Layering creates visual interest. Subtle **shadows** or **overlaps** make flat designs feel dimensional. Transparency helps layers blend, especially when using text over photos. A semi-transparent overlay can make text readable without muting the background image completely.

The key is clarity—depth should enhance, not confuse.

Creating Flow and Movement

Movement gives design rhythm. Diagonal lines or angled elements create energy. Horizontal layouts feel calm and steady.

Directional cues—arrows, icons, even the way a model's gaze points—guide the viewer. If someone in an image looks toward your product or headline, the viewer's eyes follow naturally.

Repetition builds rhythm too. Reusing shapes, lines, or colors across a layout creates a sense of continuity. It's visual storytelling—one element leads to the next until the message resolves.

Strong composition is often invisible because it works. The viewer doesn't notice the alignment, spacing, or flow—they simply understand the message. The design feels effortless, even though every inch was planned. In Canva, mastering composition isn't about templates; it's about thinking like a guide, not an artist. Lead the eye, simplify the path, and clarity will follow.

Chapter 9: Working with Templates

Working with Templates

Templates make design accessible, but they can also make everything look the same. Canva's library is full of sleek, ready-to-use layouts that attract beginners and professionals alike. Yet, scroll through social media or marketing materials and you'll often spot the same template, barely edited. The trick isn't avoiding templates—it's transforming them so thoroughly that no one can tell where you started.

Customizing Templates to Avoid Generic Looks

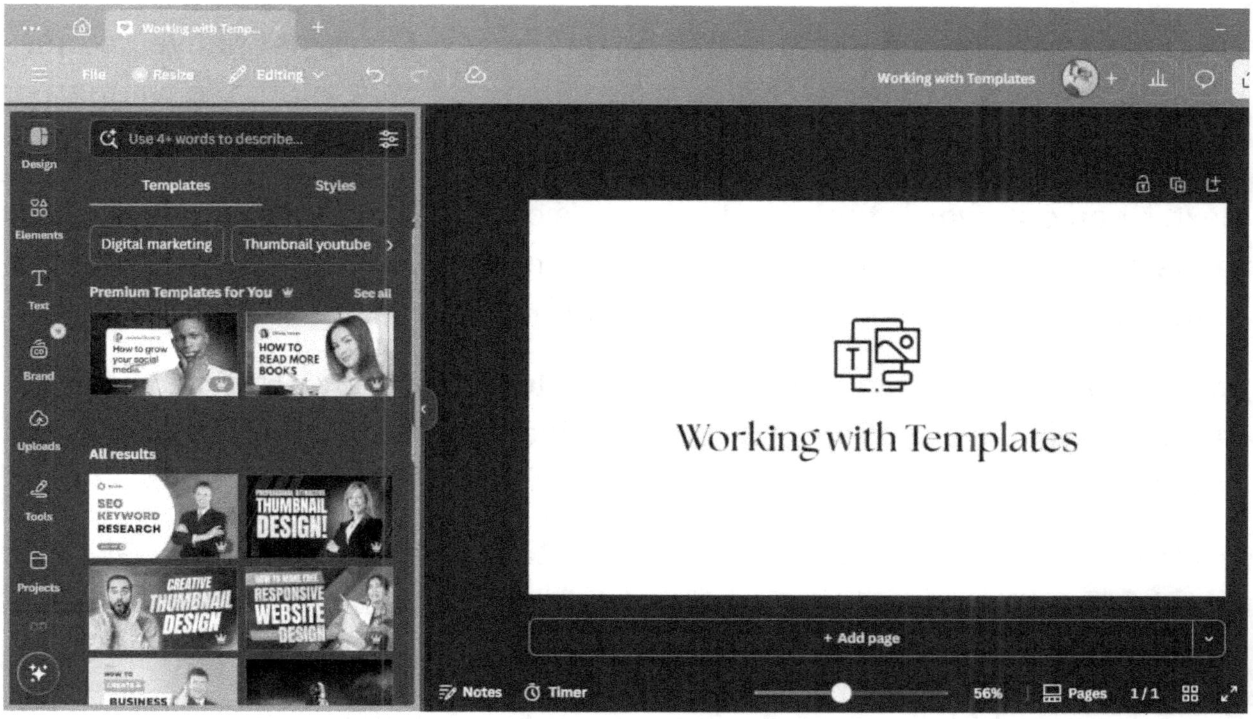

Why Templates Look Generic

Templates look generic for one simple reason: people use them without changing their visual DNA. The fonts, stock photos, and default colors are what make them instantly recognizable. Even subtle tweaks—swapping a headline or inserting a logo—don't erase the original structure.

When dozens of businesses use the same template, patterns emerge. Viewers start recognizing the layout, even subconsciously. The same gradient background or rounded photo placeholder becomes visual déjà vu.

The problem isn't the template itself—it's the shallow customization. Changing text while keeping every other element intact turns a design tool into a fill-in-the-blank exercise. The goal is to treat templates as blueprints, not finished products.

"Being inspired by a template" means understanding *why* it works: the balance, the spacing, the tone. "Copying a template" means replicating it without intention. The difference is design thinking.

Strategic Template Modification

Transforming a template starts with bold changes. Don't just nudge colors—**replace the entire palette**. Switch warm tones for cool, muted for vibrant, or pastel for monochrome. This single decision can shift the entire mood.

Next, **swap out every stock photo**. Canva's built-in images are widely used, so reuse stands out immediately. Replace them with your own product photos, brand imagery, or even solid color backgrounds with vector art.

Layouts define structure. **Rearrange the elements**. Move text boxes, resize frames, or flip the alignment. Adjusting positioning breaks the template's visual fingerprint.

Fonts carry enormous weight in personalization. Change them decisively—not just the headline but all levels of text. A new font pairing instantly redefines personality and tone.

You can also **add or remove design elements** to rebalance the layout. Delete an unnecessary shape, insert a divider line, or introduce a subtle background texture. These small shifts compound to create something distinctly yours.

Borrowing Layout Logic

The most advanced way to use templates is to study *why* they work, not just *how* they look. Every strong template has an underlying logic—balanced margins, clear hierarchy, and visual rhythm.

Use that structure as a guide. Observe how text aligns with images, where negative space appears, and how contrast draws the eye. Then apply those principles to your own blank canvas.

Sometimes, the smartest move is to **extract one element**—a clever font treatment, a layout grid, or an interesting shape arrangement—and build something new around it. That's design thinking in action: reusing logic, not copying design.

Templates are teachers if you learn to dissect them. Reverse-engineer the choices behind the visual flow, and you'll develop intuition that extends far beyond Canva.

Mixing Template Elements

A creative way to escape template repetition is to **combine multiple templates**. Take a headline treatment from one, an image frame from another, and a color scheme from a third.

This approach produces unique compositions while keeping professional structure. The key is cohesion—unify the mix with consistent fonts, color tones, and spacing.

The danger lies in mixing too many styles. A vintage font paired with a futuristic layout and corporate color palette feels disjointed. Always define your design's voice first—then let the templates serve that vision.

When done well, template blending creates something polished yet original. You're using Canva's resources, not being used by them.

When to Start from Scratch vs. Using Templates

Templates Work Best For

Templates shine when structure matters more than originality. Standard formats—resumes, business cards, flyers, social media posts—benefit from templates because they follow universal expectations.

They're also perfect for **time-sensitive projects**. If a client needs a campaign graphic in hours, starting from a professional base saves time without sacrificing quality.

Templates are also **learning tools**. Beginners can study how spacing, hierarchy, and balance work by deconstructing pre-made layouts. Even experienced designers use them to stay efficient.

For multi-design projects—like a full Instagram campaign—templates ensure **visual consistency**. Using the same underlying grid or structure across several posts maintains brand harmony while allowing creative variation.

Starting Fresh Makes Sense For

Some projects demand originality from the ground up. **Brand-specific work**—logos, pitch decks, product packaging—should reflect unique identity, not shared templates.

If your project has **unusual dimensions** or a format Canva doesn't predefine, it's faster to start from scratch. Templates lock certain proportions and design constraints that may limit creativity.

Designers with strong visual instincts often find **templates slower**, because they spend more time undoing preset elements than creating freely.

Creative experimentation also requires open space. If your concept doesn't fit any template mold, starting fresh lets you explore structure, composition, and typography without fighting against existing design logic.

The Hybrid Approach

The smartest workflow often combines both methods. **Start with a template**, then break it apart. Replace visuals, fonts, and layouts until it feels original. Think of it as remodeling a house—you're keeping the foundation, but repainting every wall and moving the furniture.

Over time, you can build **personal template libraries**. These become your design shortcuts: customized structures you've refined for your brand or clients.

You can also create **branded templates**—consistent frameworks with your fonts, colors, and layout logic. These make team collaboration smoother and ensure that all future designs align with brand identity.

Templates evolve through iteration. Each time you modify one, you learn something new about structure, rhythm, or visual storytelling. Eventually, your "templates" won't look like anyone else's—they'll look like yours.

Templates are tools, not crutches. They save time, but their real value lies in what you do after you open them. The best designers don't reject templates; they reshape them. A strong design doesn't announce, "This started as a Canva template." It says, "This works."

Chapter 10: Canva AI Tools

Canva AI Tools

Artificial intelligence in Canva handles tasks that once demanded professional tools and years of training. Background removal that once meant tedious Photoshop work now happens with a single click. AI text generation fills the silence of an empty page with workable drafts. These tools don't replace creative thinking—they amplify it. They make design faster, cleaner, and more accessible for everyone, especially beginners who want professional results without the steep learning curve.

Magic Write and Text Generation

How Magic Write Works

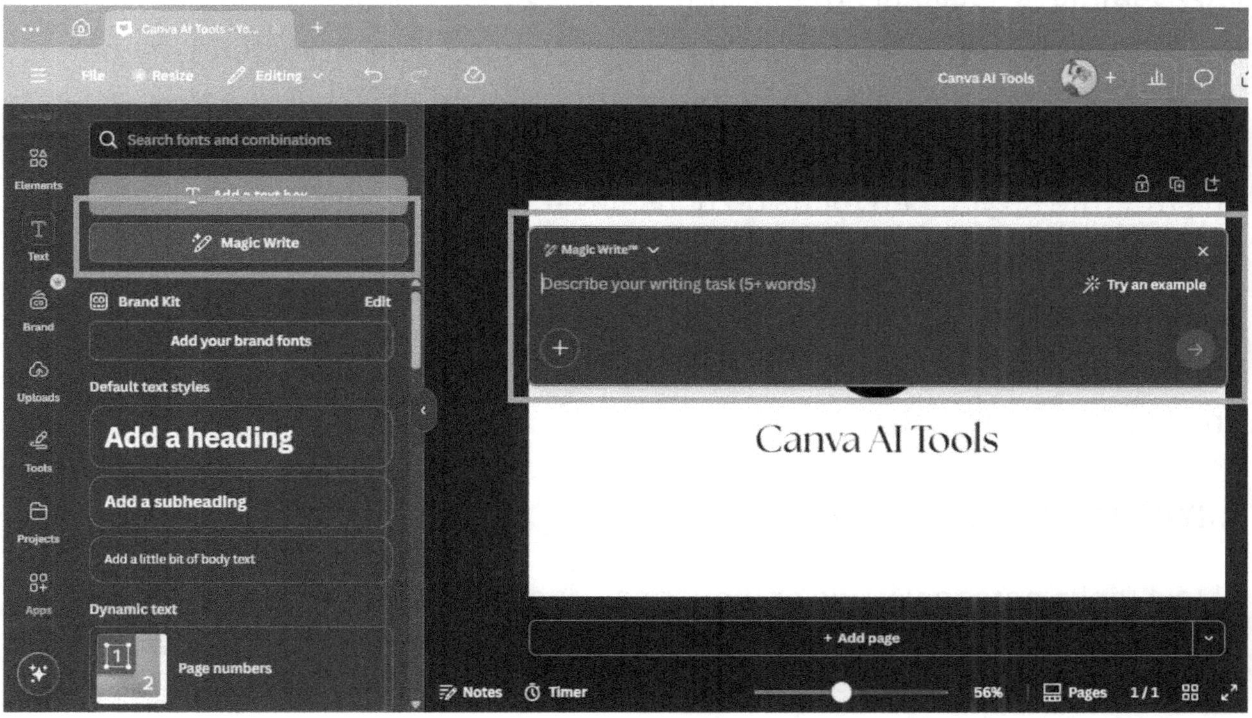

Magic Write sits inside Canva's Docs, social media templates, and other text-based projects. To activate it, you simply type "/magic write" or click the spark icon. A prompt box appears, inviting you to tell the AI what you need. The more specific your prompt, the better the output. For instance, "Write a caption for a fitness brand's Instagram post about morning workouts" produces sharper results than "Write an Instagram caption."

The system works best when you give it context—tone, purpose, and audience. It can write in styles ranging from professional to playful, though tone consistency can vary. What you get isn't a final product but a strong starting point. Some outputs are generic or repetitive, but others land surprisingly close to what you'd expect from a polished copywriter.

Practical Applications

Magic Write helps when ideas stall or when deadlines loom. You can use it to brainstorm headlines, ad taglines, or catchy one-liners. It can suggest hooks for blog posts, outline content ideas, or generate caption options for social media campaigns. Instead of staring at a blank page, you start with material you can refine.

For example, a designer creating posts for a skincare brand can ask Magic Write for "10 Instagram captions promoting hydration." The AI instantly generates options that can be edited to fit the brand's personality. It also helps generate first drafts of newsletters, product descriptions, or video scripts—saving time on structure so you can focus on polishing tone and clarity.

Magic Write is especially useful for overcoming creative blocks. When your mind feels empty, it can kickstart the process with fresh phrasing or new angles. Still, it's not a tool to depend on entirely. Think of it as a collaborator that provides raw material, not finished art.

Limitations and Editing

AI text lacks personal voice and nuance. Magic Write produces competent but neutral writing, which can sound lifeless if copied directly. You'll often need to inject brand character, adjust for accuracy, and refine the rhythm of the sentences. The AI can also produce outdated facts or overused phrases, so it's crucial to verify everything before publishing.

Use AI-generated text when you need structure or ideas quickly. Avoid it when originality or authenticity is essential—such as in personal essays, brand storytelling, or anything that reflects core identity. Magic Write is a shortcut to momentum, not a replacement for human expression.

Background Removal and Magic Eraser

Automatic Background Removal

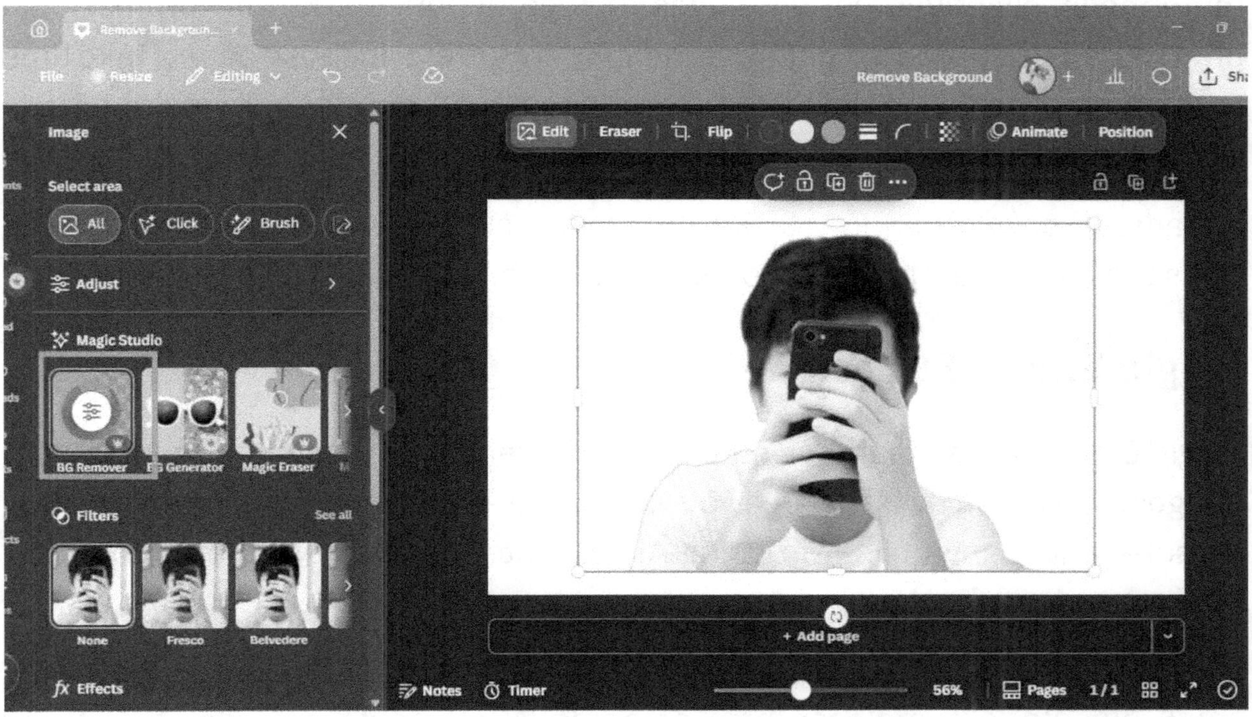

Canva's Background Remover isolates subjects automatically using AI detection. One click separates people, products, or objects from their backgrounds. The results are usually sharp, especially with clear edges or contrasting backgrounds. However, it struggles with fine details like hair, transparent materials, or complex shadows.

This tool is a favorite for product photography, professional headshots, and marketing banners. It helps create clean compositions for ads, presentations, and mockups. Once the background is removed, you can export the image with a transparent background or replace it with gradients, patterns, or branded colors.

Fixing Imperfect Removals

When the AI misses edges or leaves awkward traces, Canva provides manual brushes for refinement. You can restore or erase specific areas to tidy up outlines or fill missing parts. The cleanup process is fast, but the results depend on patience and attention to detail.

Sometimes perfection isn't necessary. For quick social graphics or small web thumbnails, slightly imperfect edges may go unnoticed. But for professional print materials or product catalogs, precision matters. In those cases, take time to refine the edges or adjust the image placement for better composition.

After removing the background, designers often add new ones—a textured wall, a gradient, or an abstract blur—to make the subject stand out. The contrast gives the image depth and a professional finish.

Magic Eraser Functionality

Magic Eraser takes cleanup a step further by removing unwanted objects from images. You brush over the area you want gone—like a power line, logo, or stray person—and Canva fills it in using AI-generated pixels from the surrounding background.

It works best on simple backgrounds such as skies, walls, or grass. Removing small objects is seamless; large or complex elements can result in blurry patches or unrealistic textures. The trick is subtlety—use Magic Eraser for light touch-ups, not major surgery.

For example, removing dust spots from a product photo or clearing distractions from a street scene usually works well. Trying to erase a large person or object from a busy background, however, can create visible distortions.

Photo Enhancement Tools

Canva's photo enhancement suite uses AI to adjust brightness, contrast, and color with one click. The "Auto Enhance" button improves lighting balance and sharpens overall image quality. It can make dull photos look crisp and professional, particularly when used on slightly underexposed or flat images.

AI upscaling improves low-resolution photos by increasing sharpness and reducing blur. This helps when working with older or smaller files that need to be used in larger formats. However, AI enhancement isn't magic—it can't fix poor composition or images that are fundamentally out of focus.

Manual control remains essential when subtlety matters. Adjusting exposure, shadows, or saturation manually often yields more natural results than relying on presets. AI enhancement works best as a quick polish, not a creative decision-maker.

When to Use AI vs. Manual Editing

AI tools excel at repetitive or technical tasks—removing backgrounds, generating ideas, or adjusting lighting. They save hours of manual work, especially during production-heavy projects. But manual editing provides precision, nuance, and control that AI can't replicate.

Learning to edit manually builds understanding of composition, color, and tone. Overreliance on AI can limit skill growth and make designs feel formulaic. The best approach is hybrid: let AI handle the grunt work, then refine manually to achieve a polished, authentic finish.

AI in Canva is a creative assistant. It speeds up workflows, removes barriers, and handles the technical grind. But the vision—the storytelling, emotion, and design intent—still comes from you.

Chapter 11: Animation and Video Features

Animation and Video Features

Static designs still dominate much of digital media, but animation has quietly become the standard. Platforms like Instagram, TikTok, and LinkedIn now reward motion over stillness. Even a simple fade or slide brings energy to an otherwise flat image. Canva's animation and video features let anyone add movement without learning complex video editing software. The challenge isn't in making things move—it's in knowing when to stop. Too much motion overwhelms; the right amount directs attention and keeps viewers engaged.

Basic Animation Tools

Page Animations

In Canva, animations are controlled from the top menu bar under the **"Animate"** option. Once selected, a panel opens showing a list of presets such as *Fade*, *Pan*, *Rise*, *Pop*, and *Slide*. Each preset creates a distinct motion effect for the entire page or design. For example, *Fade* gently brings elements into view, while *Pan* slides them in from a chosen direction.

Designers can adjust timing to control how long the animation runs. Slower animations feel smoother and more professional, while faster ones add energy. Canva's preview button makes it easy to test animations before finalizing, helping users fine-tune transitions and pacing.

Page animations are best used for presentations, video ads, or social media reels where scenes transition smoothly. They establish rhythm and guide attention, especially when layered with audio or subtle text movement.

Element Animations

Beyond entire pages, Canva allows individual elements—like text boxes, icons, and images—to move independently. You can select a specific object, click **"Animate"**, and apply entrance or exit effects. Entrance animations (such as *Pop*, *Fade In*, or *Rise*) draw attention to key content, like a headline or logo. Exit animations help cleanly transition between messages or slides.

Animating text separately from visuals allows for storytelling rhythm. For example, a product name might fade in before a tagline slides underneath. Designers can also stagger animations, setting each element to appear with a slight delay, creating a flowing sequence that feels natural.

However, animation should have intent. Highlighting key points or creating hierarchy through motion feels purposeful. Animating everything just to "look cool" makes the design chaotic.

Animation Subtlety

The line between effective and distracting animation comes down to restraint. Movement should support comprehension, not compete with it. Slow transitions communicate professionalism; fast ones can feel rushed or unrefined.

When every element on the screen moves simultaneously, nothing stands out. Strategic stillness allows motion to have meaning. For instance, a calm fade in a corporate presentation feels polished, while quick jumps might work better in upbeat social media ads.

Context defines the tone. A financial report should move with precision and minimal motion, while a fashion brand might benefit from faster, stylized animations. Subtlety ensures that viewers remember the message, not just the movement.

Creating Simple Video Content

Multi-Page Video Sequences

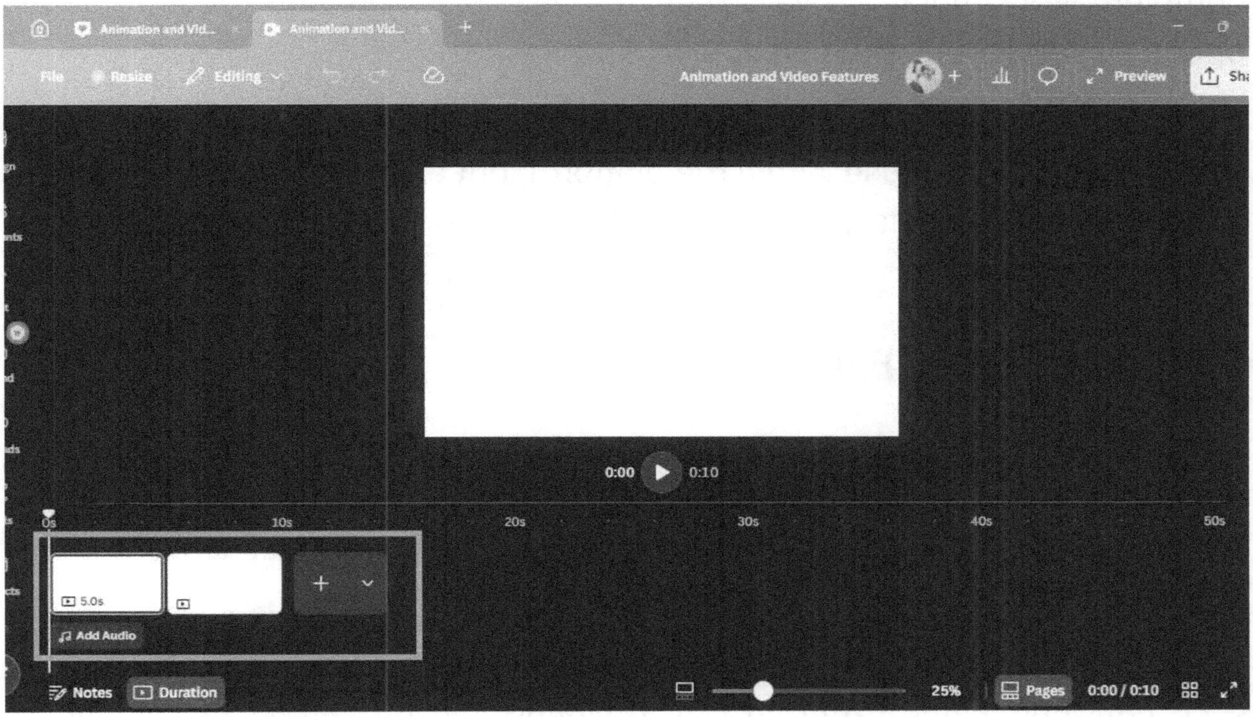

Canva treats each page of a design as a video scene. When combined, they create a timeline of clips. Each page's duration can be adjusted—shorter times for quick flashes or longer ones for more detailed visuals. You can reorder pages, duplicate them, or insert transitions like *Dissolve* or *Slide* for smooth progression.

Timing matters. Viewers should have enough time to read text and absorb images before the video cuts to the next scene. A good rhythm is typically between two and five seconds per page, depending on content density.

This system makes it easy to create short promotional videos, slideshows, tutorials, or brand intros—all without video-editing software.

Adding Music and Sound

Canva includes an audio library with tracks sorted by genre, mood, and energy level. Users can browse for background music that fits their design's tone—

calm acoustic tunes for reflections, upbeat electronic sounds for ads, or cinematic beats for storytelling.

Audio can be trimmed, faded in or out, and adjusted for volume so it complements rather than overpowers the visuals. For projects requiring sound effects or voiceovers, you can upload custom files.

It's important to pay attention to copyright restrictions. Music from Canva's library is licensed for use within the platform, but external uploads must have appropriate rights. Matching the right sound to the motion elevates the emotional impact of a video and keeps viewers engaged.

Exporting Video Files

When the video is ready, Canva exports in MP4 format—the most compatible option for social media and web uploads. Users can select resolution quality, typically between 720p for web and 1080p for professional presentations. Higher resolutions increase clarity but also file size.

Before exporting, preview the video to ensure timing, music, and animation all sync correctly. Once exported, these videos can be shared on Instagram, LinkedIn, YouTube, or embedded in websites and PowerPoint decks. The simplicity of the process turns static designs into dynamic storytelling tools.

GIFs and Motion Graphics Basics

GIFs are another way to add motion without full video production. They're short, looping animations that play automatically on most platforms—perfect for social posts, emails, and landing pages. Canva can export short animated designs as GIFs, allowing users to turn logos, icons, or quick transitions into attention-grabbing loops.

Looping is key: a well-timed GIF cycles seamlessly without a harsh reset. File size must also be managed—larger GIFs can slow down web pages or fail to load properly. Unlike MP4 videos, GIFs lack sound and have lower color quality, so they're best for quick, silent motion.

Simple motion graphics, like moving text or pulsing icons, can add life to static layouts. For example, a "Sale" badge that gently expands and contracts draws attention without distracting. Rotating elements, glowing highlights, or sliding arrows help emphasize direction and flow. The best loops feel smooth and natural rather than jarring or overly fast.

GIFs shine where subtle motion enhances clarity—showing a process step, emphasizing a call-to-action, or catching a viewer's eye in a scrolling feed. They're lightweight, automatic, and effective when used sparingly.

Animation in Canva expands what designs can do, turning flat ideas into living stories. Yet the same principles of design still apply: clarity, purpose, and restraint. Movement should enhance communication, not overshadow it. When animation supports meaning rather than distracts from it, the result feels modern, professional, and memorable.

Chapter 13: Collaborating and Sharing Designs

Collaborating and Sharing Designs

Design rarely happens in isolation. Clients want previews. Team members offer suggestions. Stakeholders request edits. Canva turns what could be a chaotic back-and-forth into an organized workflow—but only when collaboration tools are used thoughtfully. Understanding sharing permissions, feedback systems, and version management keeps projects efficient and under control.

Sharing Options and Permissions

Types of Sharing Access

Canva's sharing system revolves around levels of access. **View-only links** let others see a design without changing anything. They're ideal for client reviews or stakeholder previews, where feedback matters but edits should be restricted.

Edit access gives collaborators full control. Anyone with this permission can move, delete, or modify elements. It's powerful but risky if used loosely, especially when multiple people are editing the same project. Reserve it for trusted team members actively contributing to design execution.

Comment-only access strikes a balance. Viewers can leave feedback without altering the layout or text. This mode works best for structured reviews, especially when the person providing feedback isn't a designer.

Lastly, there's **template sharing**, which differs from project sharing. When you share a template, collaborators can use it as a base for their own designs without affecting your original. It's useful for brand kits, recurring campaigns, or training materials where consistency matters.

Link Sharing vs. Email Invitations

Canva allows two main sharing routes: **public links** and **email invitations**. Public links are fast—anyone with the link can open the file. But convenience comes at a cost. These links remain active unless manually disabled, so avoid using them for sensitive or confidential work.

Private invitations give you more control. By entering specific email addresses, you decide exactly who can access the project. It's the safer route for client deliverables or internal company work.

You can also **adjust permissions or revoke access** anytime. For projects with limited lifespans—like seasonal campaigns—set links to expire or remove collaborators once their input is complete.

Choosing between the two depends on context: public links are convenient for quick previews, while private invites protect sensitive material and maintain accountability.

Team Folders and Organization

When collaboration becomes ongoing, organization matters as much as design quality. Canva's **Team Folders** let groups manage multiple projects under one workspace. Within folders, permissions can differ—some users can edit everything, while others can only view.

Shared folders keep assets centralized: logos, color palettes, social templates, and approved images. This prevents duplication and confusion across projects.

Good folder structure is key. Create logical naming systems like "ClientName_SocialAds_Q1" or "BrandAssets_Final." Avoid dumping unrelated files together—it slows everyone down.

Proper organization keeps teams efficient, especially when managing dozens of designs across campaigns.

Real-Time Collaboration

One of Canva's most powerful features is **real-time editing**. Multiple people can open and work on the same file simultaneously. Colored cursors show who's doing what, while instant syncing ensures everyone sees the latest changes.

However, this convenience brings potential issues. Two people moving the same element or editing overlapping text can create confusion. Teams should define responsibilities before co-editing sessions—decide who handles layout, copy, or visual adjustments.

Used well, real-time collaboration accelerates progress. Used carelessly, it can overwrite good work. Communication makes the difference.

Gathering and Incorporating Feedback

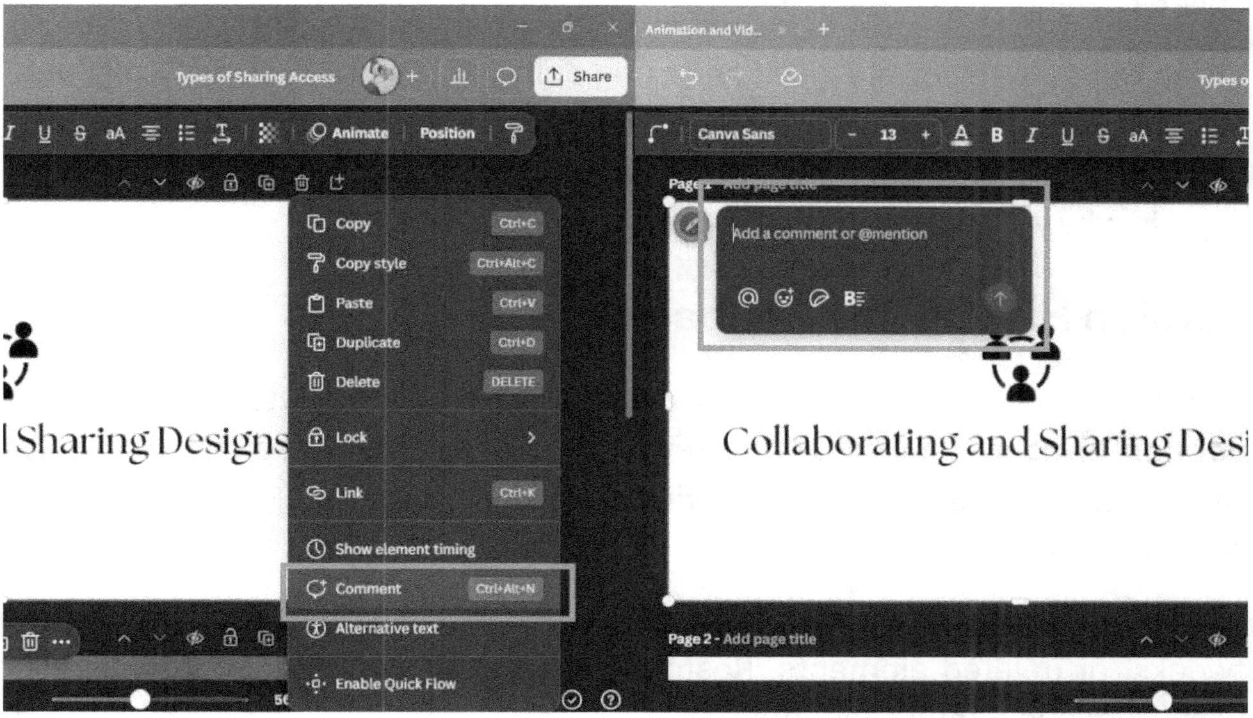

The Comment System

Feedback works best when it's specific, and Canva's **commenting tools** make that possible. Comments attach directly to elements—text boxes, images, shapes—so reviewers can point out exactly what needs adjustment.

Using **@mentions**, collaborators can direct notes to specific people ("@Alex can you check alignment here?"). Each comment becomes part of a threaded discussion, keeping context intact. Once an issue is addressed, comments can be marked as **resolved**, decluttering the workspace.

This structure prevents long, messy email chains. Feedback stays where it belongs—inside the design.

Feedback Workflow

Productive collaboration isn't just about tools—it's about process. Before sharing, define what type of feedback you want. Are you looking for layout input, content edits, or general impressions? Clear expectations prevent vague or conflicting comments.

Set **review deadlines** to keep projects moving. Without them, designs can linger in "pending feedback" limbo.

When multiple reviewers give conflicting opinions, use your design judgment. Not every suggestion improves the final product. Balance stakeholder requests with visual and brand consistency. If feedback undermines clarity or structure, explain why your approach works better.

Version History and Rollback

Even with structure, collaboration means revisions. Canva automatically saves **version history**, allowing you to revisit or restore earlier designs. Accessing these versions helps when an experiment goes wrong or a stakeholder wants to "go back to the last version."

Version comparisons reveal exactly what changed—color adjustments, layout tweaks, or deleted elements. Restoring takes just one click, protecting your work from accidental overwrites.

This feature makes experimentation safer. Designers can explore bold ideas knowing they can always revert.

Exporting for External Review

Not everyone reviewing a design will use Canva. For those outside the platform, export options bridge the gap. You can send **PDFs or image files** for easy viewing, preserving design integrity while preventing edits.

For more visual presentations, use **mockups** to show designs in real-world contexts—like business cards on a desk or social posts on a phone screen. Canva's **presentation mode** is also ideal for walking clients through a design live, especially during remote reviews.

If feedback happens outside Canva, third-party **annotation tools** like PDF editors or commenting platforms can complement your workflow. The key is to keep communication clear and centralized, whether it happens inside or outside Canva.

Chapter 14: Downloading and Exporting Your Work

Downloading and Exporting Your Work

Creating the design is only half the job. Getting it out of Canva in the right format, at the right quality, for the right purpose completes the work. Export settings might look technical, but they're the bridge between what looks great on screen and what performs correctly once shared or printed. Choosing wrong can lead to blurry prints, oversized files, or colors that look nothing like what you designed.

Choosing the Right File Formats

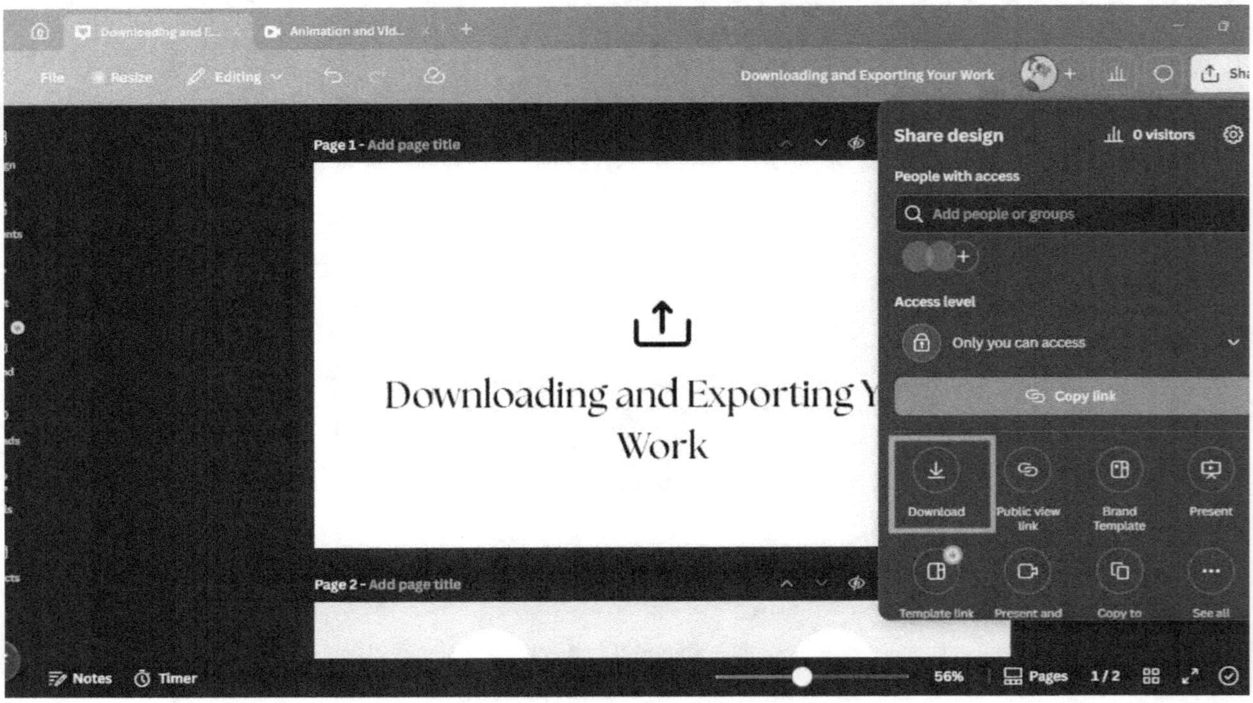

Canva offers several export options, each serving a specific purpose. The best format depends on where your design will live—on a website, in print, in a presentation, or as part of a video.

PNG: The Versatile Default

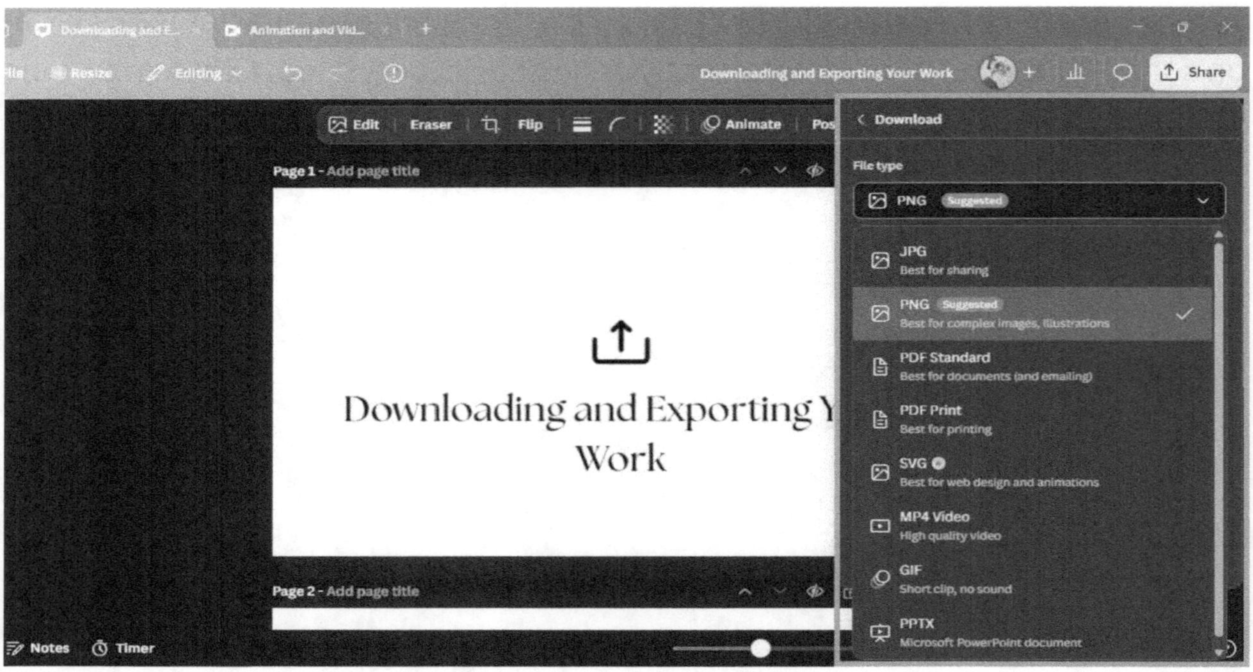

PNG files preserve image quality and support transparent backgrounds, which makes them ideal for designs with logos, text overlays, or graphics that need to sit over colored or photographic backgrounds. Because PNGs don't use lossy compression, every detail stays crisp—edges of icons, fine text, and layered visuals all hold up well.

The tradeoff is file size. PNGs are heavier than JPGs, which can slow down web pages or increase storage needs if you export large batches. Use PNGs for digital graphics where clarity and transparency matter more than file size.

JPG: For Photos and Web Use

JPG files balance quality with efficiency. They compress images to make them smaller and faster to load, which is perfect for online content. The downside is compression artifacts—those small, fuzzy patches or blurring that appear when quality is reduced too far.

JPGs don't support transparency, so backgrounds are always solid. Still, for social media, email newsletters, or blog posts where images must load quickly, JPGs are a practical choice. Use a high-quality export for hero images and reduce quality for secondary visuals to save space.

PDF: For Print and Documents

PDF is the professional standard for anything that will be printed or distributed as a document. It preserves layout, fonts, and images exactly as they appear in Canva. Printers prefer PDFs because they embed fonts and flatten layers, preventing unwanted changes.

Canva offers **Standard PDF** and **PDF Print**. Standard PDFs are lighter, ideal for digital sharing. PDF Print files retain the highest quality and color precision, designed for physical printing. Multi-page exports—like brochures or reports—are handled seamlessly as a single PDF document. When sending to a professional printer, always choose **PDF Print** for sharp, color-accurate output.

SVG: For Scalable Graphics

SVG (Scalable Vector Graphics) files shine when you need infinite scalability—logos, icons, or any simple shape-based design. Unlike PNG or JPG, SVGs are vector-based, meaning they stay sharp no matter how large or small they're displayed.

They're not ideal for photos or detailed textures since those rely on pixels, not paths. But for digital interfaces or brand assets that must adapt across different screen sizes, SVG is unbeatable. They also perform well on websites, with smaller file sizes and faster loading times.

MP4 and GIF: For Motion

If you've added animation to your Canva design, export options expand to **MP4 video** or **GIF**. MP4 offers smoother playback, full-color range, and better compression, making it the preferred choice for most platforms.

GIFs, on the other hand, loop endlessly and don't require a play button, but they're limited to 256 colors and can balloon in file size quickly. Use GIFs for short, looping social posts or visual effects. For anything longer or more complex, export as MP4. Some social media platforms—like Instagram and LinkedIn—favor MP4 for quality and consistency.

Resolution and Quality Considerations

Resolution determines how sharp your exported design looks. It's about how many pixels fit into each inch of your design. The higher the density, the clearer the result.

Understanding DPI and PPI

Canva usually exports files at web-friendly resolutions, but understanding DPI (dots per inch) and PPI (pixels per inch) helps you make the right call.

- **72 DPI** is standard for screens—good enough for social media, websites, and presentations.

- **300 DPI** is the benchmark for print—anything less can look pixelated when physically produced.

High-resolution files take longer to export and result in larger sizes, but they're worth it for professional printing.

Balancing Quality and File Size

Not every project needs maximum quality. For a banner ad or Instagram post, a smaller file loads faster and performs better. For large-format prints or product packaging, always prioritize clarity over file size.

If your exported files are huge, experiment with Canva's **compression** options. Export a version at slightly lower quality and compare it side by side—you'll often find the difference invisible to the naked eye, but with a much smaller file size.

Cropping and Dimensions at Export

You can export entire projects or specific pages from multi-page documents. Canva also allows **custom dimensions**, which helps when you need a particular size for a platform or print layout.

Be cautious when resizing. Stretching or shrinking without maintaining aspect ratio can distort your design. Whenever possible, design at the final dimensions instead of adjusting during export. Use export resizing only for small adjustments or quick reformatting.

Color Profile Considerations

Colors can shift between screen and print because each uses different color models.

- **sRGB** is for screens—what you see on Canva, your phone, or your laptop.
- **CMYK** is for printers—how ink mixes on paper.

Canva primarily exports in sRGB, though **PDF Print** exports often simulate CMYK for more accurate results. If your printed output looks duller or more muted than expected, this is likely a color profile mismatch, not a design flaw.

Monitors also vary in color calibration, so what looks perfect on one screen may appear warmer or cooler on another. Always test-print if color accuracy is critical.

Matching Export Settings to Purpose

Every design has a destination. Optimizing exports means thinking ahead about where the file will live.

- **For social media**: JPG or PNG at 72 DPI. Keep file size small for fast uploads.
- **For presentations**: PDF (Standard) or PNG. Prioritize clarity without massive file sizes.
- **For print**: PDF Print at 300 DPI. Confirm dimensions match your printer's specs.
- **For logos or scalable assets**: SVG. Ensure colors match your brand palette.
- **For motion**: MP4 for smooth animation and easy sharing.

A design made for Instagram won't hold up on a billboard, and a 300-DPI print-ready file is unnecessary for an email attachment. Each format serves its purpose—choosing the right one ensures your design performs exactly as intended.

Chapter 15: Troubleshooting Common Issues

Troubleshooting Common Issues

Even straightforward software throws curveballs. Images won't upload. Layouts shift unexpectedly. Fonts disappear. Elements refuse to align. Troubleshooting isn't about fixing every possible problem—it's about knowing where to look when things go wrong. Canva runs smoothly most of the time, but when it doesn't, understanding the usual culprits saves hours of frustration.

Uploading and Importing Problems

File Format Incompatibility

Canva supports most common file types, including **JPG, PNG, SVG, GIF, and PDF**. However, not all image formats are created equal. If you're trying to upload something like a **TIFF, HEIC, or RAW file**, Canva may reject it. These formats are often camera-native or platform-specific and require conversion first.

Sometimes files fail because they're **corrupted**—a download interrupted midway or a transfer gone wrong can make a file unreadable. Opening the image in another program (like Paint or Preview) and re-saving it as a standard PNG or JPG usually solves the problem.

There's also a **size limit** to uploads. Extremely large files—especially high-resolution photos or long PDFs—can exceed Canva's capacity. Compressing them using tools like TinyPNG or re-exporting at lower quality typically helps.

Image Quality Issues After Upload

If an image looks blurry after uploading, the issue usually lies with the original file, not Canva. Low-resolution photos remain low-resolution no matter where they're uploaded. Canva can't create detail that isn't there.

For best results, start with images at least **2,000 pixels wide** for web use and much higher for print. Canva applies mild compression to uploaded images to balance performance and storage efficiency. This can cause small quality drops, especially on large screens. When image clarity is critical, test exports at multiple resolutions before finalizing.

Font Upload Failures

Canva lets you upload custom fonts, but not every font works seamlessly. Some fail due to **licensing restrictions**—certain commercial fonts prohibit third-party uploads. Others may be in the wrong format; Canva accepts **OTF, TTF, and WOFF** files only.

If a font still won't upload, check whether it's properly installed on your system or try a free equivalent from Canva's built-in library. Often, Canva's native fonts are optimized for its rendering engine, ensuring smoother exports and fewer layout glitches.

Fixing Layout Glitches and Missing Elements

Elements Won't Move or Resize

When elements refuse to budge, they're usually **locked**. Canva's lock feature prevents accidental movement during editing. Unlocking is simple—select the element and click the **unlock icon** in the toolbar.

Sometimes elements are part of a **group**, which means you can't move one without moving the others. Ungroup them first to regain individual control. Another common issue is **layer order**—an element may be hiding behind another. Use the **Position tool** to bring it forward.

Text Boxes Behaving Strangely

Text boxes in Canva can auto-adjust size or stay fixed, depending on settings. If text disappears mid-sentence, you may be using a fixed-size box without enough room. Expand the box manually or enable auto-resize.

Overflow issues often cause partial text visibility, while unexpected spacing or line breaks come from hidden formatting. Select all text and reset spacing to defaults if it looks uneven.

When custom fonts fail to load, Canva substitutes them automatically. This can alter line breaks or alignment. If you notice your layout shifting unexpectedly, check whether a font substitution occurred.

Alignment Issues

Canva's alignment guides and "snap" system help keep elements in line—but sometimes they work against you. If snapping feels inaccurate, zoom in for more control or temporarily disable snap-to-grid for manual placement.

Elements occasionally align to the wrong object due to **layering order**. Reorder elements using the Arrange menu, or lock background layers to avoid unwanted snapping.

Precision work—like spacing icons evenly—requires higher zoom levels. Tiny misalignments invisible at 50% become obvious when printed or exported. Always zoom in to double-check before exporting.

Disappearing Elements

If something suddenly vanishes, don't panic. Most of the time, it's not gone—it's just **moved off-canvas** or hidden behind another layer.

Use **Ctrl/Cmd + Z** to undo recent moves or open the **Version History** panel to restore an earlier version. Transparency settings can also make items invisible; if something seems missing, check its **opacity** level.

Performance and Loading Issues

Slow Loading and Lag

Large, image-heavy projects or designs with hundreds of elements can slow Canva down. Each item—photo, shape, or text box—adds memory load.

To fix lag, simplify the design by merging layers, reducing high-resolution images, or breaking complex projects into smaller pages. Clearing your **browser cache** can also improve performance.

If Canva still lags, check your **internet connection**. Since Canva runs in the cloud, unstable connections can cause freezing or slow uploads.

Autosave Failures

Canva autosaves continuously, but it relies on an active internet connection. If the **saving indicator** shows "offline" or "changes not saved," your edits may be at risk.

Try refreshing the page once your connection stabilizes. Canva usually restores unsaved changes automatically. For added safety, manually **duplicate the design** occasionally as a backup copy.

Canvas Freezing or Crashing

Browser compatibility matters. Canva generally runs best on **Google Chrome**, though it also supports Firefox and Safari. Running multiple tabs or heavy browser extensions can cause slowdowns or crashes.

If Canva freezes, try refreshing before force-quitting. Restarting the browser often resolves temporary memory issues. Older devices with limited RAM may struggle with complex designs—closing background applications can help free resources.

Mobile App vs. Desktop Experience

Feature Differences

The **mobile app** is excellent for quick edits but lacks some of the advanced tools available on desktop. Features like custom font uploads, detailed spacing adjustments, and certain animation effects may be missing or simplified.

The mobile interface is designed for convenience—ideal for posting social content or making small tweaks—but not for heavy layout work. For large projects, the **desktop version** provides more control and precision.

Web Browser vs. Desktop Application

Canva's **web app** runs directly in browsers and offers universal access from any device. The **desktop application**, available for Windows and macOS, can feel smoother since it uses system resources directly instead of browser memory.

However, both versions require internet access for saving and syncing. The desktop app may offer partial offline support, but features like asset uploads and collaboration still need a connection.

If designs don't appear synced between devices, give them a few minutes—cloud syncing can lag briefly.

Touch Interface Challenges

Touchscreens, especially on phones, make fine adjustments difficult. Moving small icons or text precisely with a finger is tricky. Tablets improve usability with styluses, but desktop setups with a mouse and keyboard remain best for exact work.

On mobile, use **zoom gestures** and grid snapping to refine placement. For anything requiring detailed spacing, switch back to desktop to finish the job.

Cross-Device Workflow

Canva's cloud system allows seamless transitions between devices. You can start a design on desktop, review it on mobile, and finalize it on a tablet.

Edits sync automatically, though it's smart to double-check before exporting—especially if fonts or elements appear missing after device switches. Designs created on one platform should display correctly on another, provided all assets (fonts, images) are available.

Common Export Problems

Export Failures

Exports can fail due to **file size, unstable connections, or timeout issues**. If a design won't download, try exporting at lower resolution or breaking it into smaller parts. For multi-page documents, export pages in batches to reduce load.

Some browsers block downloads automatically. Check your **download settings** or pop-up permissions if exports never start.

Unexpected Results After Export

Sometimes the exported version doesn't match what you saw in Canva. Color shifts occur due to **RGB vs. CMYK** differences between screen and print. Lower resolution or compression settings can also blur text or images.

If fonts appear missing in PDFs, make sure you're exporting with **"Embed fonts"** enabled or use Canva's native fonts. Transparency problems—such as unwanted white backgrounds—often come from exporting in the wrong format. PNG handles transparency best.

File Compatibility

When exported files won't open elsewhere, it's usually a **software mismatch**. Some older programs can't read modern PDF or SVG standards. Re-export in a simpler format like JPG or Standard PDF.

If a client can't open your design, ask what software they're using and adjust accordingly. Re-exporting in a compatible format usually fixes the problem.

Chapter 16: Tips and Tricks for Better Designs

Tips and Tricks for Better Designs

Experience teaches shortcuts. Designers develop muscle memory for efficient workflows. They recognize patterns in what works and what doesn't. These accumulated insights separate beginners from proficient users—not talent, but knowledge of the small adjustments that compound into significantly better results.

Keyboard Shortcuts and Efficiency Tips

Essential Shortcuts

Canva isn't just about creativity—it's about speed. Learning shortcuts builds momentum and keeps you in flow. The most important ones are simple: **copy (Ctrl/Cmd+C)**, **paste (Ctrl/Cmd+V)**, **undo (Ctrl/Cmd+Z)**, and **redo (Ctrl/Cmd+Shift+Z)**. These alone can cut minutes from repetitive edits.

Grouping elements (**Ctrl/Cmd+G**) helps move multiple objects as one. Ungrouping (**Ctrl/Cmd+Shift+G**) restores flexibility when you need to adjust individual pieces. For layering, use **Ctrl/Cmd+]** to bring elements forward and **Ctrl/Cmd+[** to send them back. These small commands save constant trips to the toolbar.

Zoom shortcuts—**Ctrl/Cmd + or -**—make precision work smoother. Zooming out offers perspective on balance and spacing; zooming in helps align text and shapes perfectly.

Speed Techniques

Efficiency isn't about rushing—it's about reducing repetition. Duplicating an entire design lets you create variations without starting from scratch. A campaign can branch into multiple formats in minutes by simply cloning and adjusting.

Brand kits and saved palettes eliminate the need to reselect colors or fonts every time. Once a look is established, reuse it consistently. Template creation follows the same principle—set up reusable layouts for recurring projects like reports or Instagram posts.

Batch editing also saves time. Adjusting headers, footers, or color schemes across multiple pages simultaneously ensures consistency without extra effort.

Workflow Organization

Creative clutter slows everyone down. Establishing folder structures—by client, project, or campaign—keeps designs accessible. Use clear naming conventions that include **dates, project titles, and version numbers**.

Archiving completed projects frees up workspace and speeds up loading times. Star frequently used designs so you can jump into them instantly. Efficient organization means more time spent designing, less time searching.

Practical Design Hacks

Quick Visual Improvements

Good design often comes down to restraint. Limiting color palettes to **three or four colors** instantly adds polish. Increasing **line spacing** between text blocks creates airiness and legibility.

Adding **subtle shadows** or light gradients gives depth without clutter. Alignment is another silent improvement—when every element lines up cleanly, even simple layouts look intentional and professional.

Working with Limited Resources

Free Canva users can still produce professional-quality work by thinking creatively. Adjusting the **color, opacity, or rotation** of free elements can make them feel unique. Combining basic shapes—circles, triangles, rectangles—can create icons, graphs, or even characters.

Photo filters unify mismatched images. Applying the same tone or warmth to all photos ties them together visually. Clever text treatments—like overlapping letters or layering text over semi-transparent shapes—add flair without custom fonts.

Solving Common Design Problems

Text over photos is a frequent struggle. Use **semi-transparent overlays**, blurred backgrounds, or color blocks to restore readability.

For color clashes, desaturate one color or use neutral tones to soften contrast. When layouts feel text-heavy, introduce whitespace and icons to break up content.

Dry data can be made engaging with **visual hierarchy**—emphasize key numbers using size or color. The trick is to make the eye travel naturally from most important to least.

Repurposing Content

Canva's "resize" feature makes content adaptable. A single social post can become a flyer, story, or presentation slide with adjusted dimensions.

Reuse assets from old projects—icons, headers, backgrounds—to maintain consistency across campaigns. Build **design systems** with recurring styles and layouts so every new project starts halfway done.

Refresh old designs seasonally by updating colors or swapping imagery. The foundation remains the same, saving effort while keeping things current.

Advanced Composition Tricks

Visual rhythm makes a design feel balanced. Odd numbers—three photos, five icons—look more natural than even groupings.

Diagonal compositions add movement and energy, while **intentional asymmetry** feels modern when paired with balance in spacing or color weight.

Negative space isn't empty—it's functional. The shapes between elements can form patterns or lead the viewer's eye. Sometimes what you leave blank matters more than what you fill.

Avoiding Common Beginner Mistakes

Typography Pitfalls

Typography can elevate or ruin a design. Using more than two or three fonts creates visual chaos. Choose one for headlines, another for body text, and maybe a third for accents.

Text that's too small is another common flaw. If viewers have to squint, they'll stop reading. Contrast matters too—avoid light text on light backgrounds or dark on dark.

Center-alignment can make designs look amateurish, especially with long text. Left alignment feels cleaner and easier to read. All caps work for short headings, but not paragraphs—it kills readability.

Color Mistakes

Too many colors overwhelm the eye. Pick a dominant tone and two supporting ones. Complementary colors (opposites on the color wheel) create strong contrast, while analogous colors (side-by-side hues) feel harmonious.

Be mindful of **color psychology**. Bright red feels urgent; blue conveys calm and trust. Over-saturated palettes often look harsh. Subtlety usually wins.

Always check **contrast ratios** for text. Poor contrast can make designs unreadable, especially on mobile.

Layout Errors

Every design needs breathing room. Cluttered compositions with no spacing exhaust viewers. Add margins and padding to let elements breathe.

Alignment keeps structure. Misaligned text or inconsistent spacing distracts instantly. Establish invisible grids to guide placement.

Avoid competing focal points. If everything screams for attention, nothing stands out. Decide what the design should say first and make that element dominant.

Ignoring margins—placing text too close to edges—creates an unbalanced, unprofessional look.

Image Issues

Low-resolution or stretched images ruin credibility. Always use high-quality, correctly proportioned photos. Keep the **aspect ratio** consistent to avoid distortion.

Stock photos that look staged break authenticity. Look for natural, candid imagery instead. Consistent image style—either all realistic or all illustrated—creates cohesion.

Crop strategically. Focus on the subject and avoid cutting through important parts like faces or text.

General Design Missteps

Following every new trend isn't strategy—it's noise. Use trends as inspiration, not templates. Over-designing is another trap. Too many effects—drop shadows, outlines, gradients—dilute impact.

Always design for the audience, not personal taste. A poster for a children's event should feel playful; a corporate deck should feel precise and calm.

Inconsistency between designs—fonts, colors, or tone—makes brands look disorganized. Cohesion builds trust.

Above all, remember the **purpose** of design: communication. Beautiful work that doesn't deliver the message has failed, no matter how polished it looks.

Chapter 17: Resources and Next Steps

Finishing this guide marks the beginning, not the end. Design skills grow through consistent practice, observation, and curiosity. Canva keeps evolving with new tools and features, and design trends shift faster than most people realize. What separates competent designers from excellent ones isn't raw talent—it's a steady commitment to learning and experimenting.

Further Learning and Tutorials

Official Canva Resources

Canva offers a range of built-in learning tools that help users at every level sharpen their skills. The **Canva Design School** includes structured courses and step-by-step lessons covering topics from basic layout techniques to brand identity design. Each lesson is hands-on, using real projects that teach both theory and practical execution.

Video tutorials on Canva's YouTube channel walk through specific features like animation, layering, and advanced text effects. Watching how experienced designers build from scratch helps bridge the gap between theory and workflow.

Browsing Canva's **template library** is also a form of education. Every professional template demonstrates principles of alignment, contrast, and spacing. Studying how these templates are structured—how fonts and colors are balanced, how imagery supports the message—can teach design fundamentals faster than any textbook.

Practice Projects

Improvement comes through repetition and experimentation. Create **personal projects** regularly, even if they have no client or deadline. Redesign old work to see how your style evolves. Build fictional brand campaigns or social media graphics. Each attempt refines your eye for composition, typography, and balance.

Try **challenge prompts** like “Design a poster in 10 minutes” or “Redesign a brand you admire.” Constraints push creativity. Another effective exercise is **recreating professional designs** you find online. This isn’t about copying—it’s about deconstructing what makes a design work, then rebuilding it to understand the logic behind spacing, color, and visual rhythm.

Over time, these practice projects can form the foundation of a **portfolio**. Even if the designs aren’t for real clients, they showcase your progress, style, and versatility.

Canva Communities and Support

Online Communities

Learning accelerates when you’re surrounded by others who share your interest. Several **Canva-focused Facebook groups** and **Reddit communities** allow users to share their work, ask for feedback, and troubleshoot problems. Discord servers and online forums provide real-time conversations and often feature experienced designers offering guidance or critique.

Seeing how other users approach similar challenges provides valuable perspective. You’ll start noticing diverse design styles, clever techniques, and creative solutions you might not have discovered alone.

Getting Help

Canva also maintains an extensive **Help Center**, filled with searchable articles that explain nearly every feature and troubleshooting step. When something goes wrong—like a font not loading or an image failing to export—the Help Center often has the answer.

For more complex issues, **Canva’s official support team** handles user inquiries directly. They can assist with account problems, billing questions, or bugs that can’t be fixed locally. Community forums are another great place for problem-solving—experienced users often share workarounds or hidden settings that don't appear in official documentation.

Inspiration Sources

Design inspiration fuels growth. Sites like **Dribbble** and **Behance** showcase professional portfolios across styles and industries. Browsing these platforms helps you stay in tune with emerging aesthetics and trends.

Pinterest is equally valuable for collecting and organizing ideas. Create boards for color palettes, layout inspirations, or typography examples. Curating inspiration trains your eye to recognize balance and flow.

Offline, inspiration exists everywhere—billboards, magazines, packaging, and websites. Pay attention to how real-world designs guide the viewer's attention or communicate tone through spacing and color.

Staying Current

Canva frequently updates its tools, so keeping up with new features ensures your workflow stays efficient. Following Canva's **official blog**, **newsletter**, or **social media pages** provides early notice of changes or beta features.

Design trends move quickly. Bold typography might dominate one year; minimalist gradients might define the next. While it's useful to experiment with what's popular, the most effective designers blend trend awareness with timeless principles of clarity and balance.

Experimentation remains the best teacher. Test new features when they launch. Combine techniques you haven't tried before. Every project you create builds on the last, refining your intuition and understanding of what works.

Design mastery doesn't come from shortcuts—it comes from consistent effort and curiosity. Canva provides the tools, but skill comes from how you use them. Keep learning, keep experimenting, and keep refining. The foundation is here; what you build next depends entirely on your creativity and persistence.

BONUS

How to Apply for Canva for Education: A Step-by-Step Guide for Beginners

Canva for Education is a free, premium version of Canva designed for teachers, students, and educational organizations. It gives you access to all the paid features of Canva, including templates, designs, and advanced tools, to make learning and teaching visually engaging and interactive.

Here's how you can apply for **Canva for Education**:

Step 1: Visit the Canva for Education Website

- Go to Canva for Education.
- This page is dedicated to helping educators and students sign up for free access to Canva's premium features.

Step 2: Sign Up for a Canva Account

- If you don't already have a Canva account, click on **Sign up** at the top-right of the page.
- You can sign up using your **Google**, **Facebook**, or **Apple** account, or you can use your **email address** to create an account.
- If you already have a Canva account, you can **log in** using your existing credentials.

Step 3: Choose Your Role

On the sign-up page for Canva for Education, you'll be asked to specify your role:

- **Teacher**: If you're an educator in a school or academic institution.
- **Student**: If you're a student (note: you may need a school email address).
- **School Administrator**: If you're responsible for managing accounts at your institution.

Step 4: Verify Your Educational Status

Canva will ask you to verify your educational role.

Teachers: You'll need to provide information about your school (e.g., name, location, etc.) and verify your educator status.

Students: If you're a student, you'll need to provide your school email address or have your teacher invite you to join through their Canva for Education account.

Pro Tip: If you're not using a school email address, Canva may ask for additional verification, such as a school ID or proof of enrollment.

Step 5: Fill Out the Application Form

After selecting your role and verifying your status, you'll be asked to complete a form that includes your:

Full name

Educational institution details (e.g., school name, type, etc.)

Your teaching or student role

Step 6: Wait for Approval

Once you've completed the application, Canva will review your submission. This usually takes a few business days.

You'll receive an email notification once your **Canva for Education** account has been approved. After approval, you'll get free access to Canva's premium features, and you can start using Canva for your educational projects.

Step 7: Start Using Canva for Education

- After getting approved, you can start designing using all the premium features available to educators.
- You can explore a wide range of **templates, interactive content**, and **collaboration tools** tailored to educational use.
- If you're a teacher, you can share designs with your students, create engaging presentations, or design worksheets and resources.